# Polish Return Migration after Brexit

D1741650

This book explores the attitudes of Polish migrants towards the United Kingdom's departure from the European Union and considers possible return migration trajectories that may result. Based on quantitative sociological research conducted in Britain, it investigates the perceptions of Polish people in Britain and asks what they consider the likely consequences of Brexit to be for their personal, family, and professional lives, the central question being the dilemma of whether to remain abroad or return to Poland. A multifaceted approach to understanding the views of a significant migrant group when presented with considerable social and economic changes, *Polish Return Migration after Brexit* also offers forecasts of likely outcomes for institutions involved with Polish migrants and employers in Poland. It will therefore appeal to scholars of sociology and geography with interests in migration and diaspora studies, as well as to those working in the field of migration policy.

**Marek Wodawski** has a Ph.D. in Sociology and is an assistant professor at the Catholic University of Lublin, Poland. He conducts his research in the fields of Catholic social teaching, economic ethics, migration studies, sociology of nation, and national identity.

**Stanisław Fel** is a sociology professor at the Catholic University of Lublin, Poland. His research interests focus mostly on migration studies and ethical aspects of social problems.

**Jarosław Kozak** has a Ph.D. in Sociology, an assistant professor at the Catholic University of Lublin, Poland. His scientific interests revolve around quantitative research methodologies within the issues of migration studies, sociology of religion, and morality (attitude dynamics).

# Studies in Migration and Diaspora

Studies in Migration and Diaspora is a series designed to showcase the interdisciplinary and multidisciplinary nature of research in this important field. Volumes in the series cover local, national and global issues and engage with both historical and contemporary events. The books will appeal to scholars, students and all those engaged in the study of migration and diaspora. Amongst the topics covered are minority ethnic relations, transnational movements and the cultural, social and political implications of moving from 'over there', to 'over here'.

**Series Editor:**
Anne J. Kershen, Queen Mary University of London, UK

**Migration and Families in East and North Europe:**
Translocal Lifelines
*Laura Assmuth, Marit Aure, Marina Hakkarainen and Pihla Maria Siim*

**Migrant Narratives**
Storytelling as Agency, Belonging and Community
*Edited by Brigitte Bönisch-Brednich, Anastasia Christou, Silke Meyer, Marie Johanna Karner, and Anton Jakob Escher*

**Polish Immigrant Organisations in Germany**
The Transnational Opportunity Structure
*Michał Nowosielski*

**Social Media in the Lives of Young Connected Migrants**
Making and Unmaking Boundaries
*Xinyu Zhao*

**Polish Return Migration after Brexit**
A Sociological Forecast
*Marek Wodawski, Stanisław Fel and Jarosław Kozak*

For more information about this series, please visit:
https://www.routledge.com/sociology/series/ASHSER1049

# Polish Return Migration after Brexit

## A Sociological Forecast

Marek Wodawski, Stanisław Fel and Jarosław Kozak

Routledge
Taylor & Francis Group

LONDON AND NEW YORK

First published 2024
by Routledge
4 Park Square, Milton Park, Abingdon, Oxon OX14 4RN

and by Routledge
605 Third Avenue, New York, NY 10158

*Routledge is an imprint of the Taylor & Francis Group, an informa business*

© 2024 Marek Wodawski, Stanisław Fel and Jarosław Kozak

*British Library Cataloguing-in-Publication Data*
A catalogue record for this book is available from the British Library

ISBN: 9781032583822 (hbk)
ISBN: 9781032583839 (pbk)
ISBN: 9781003449843 (ebk)

DOI: 10.4324/9781003449843

Typeset in Times New Roman
by Deanta Global Publishing Services, Chennai, India

# Table of Contents

# List of Figures

# List of Tables

# Series Editor's Foreword

On 24 June 2016, the population of the United Kingdom woke up to learn that, by a narrow margin of 4%, the nation's electorate had voted to exit (Brexit) the European Union.[1] At midnight on the 31 January 2020 the divorce came into operation. Whilst there may have been a very small number of British citizens for whom the cutting of the cord with Europe might have encouraged departure from their home country, for immigrants living in Britain the outcome of the vote posed a life changing question: should we stay or should we leave? For European migrants the answer was further coloured by a emotional concern: should we remain in a country that doesn't appear to want to be linked to ours, or, in other words, "does the United Kingdom want us?"[2]

At the time, the Polish community was the largest in the United Kingdom of non-British nationality.[3] Following the announcement of the result of the Brexit vote the authors of this book, all Polish themselves, carried out a sociological survey in three cities in England – London, Oxford, and Swindon – in order to elicit what the impact of the vote had been on Polish people living in Britain. The research took place in 2019 and, though this was before Brexit actually came into operation, the authors were keen to determine in advance how Poles viewed their future in the United Kingdom in light of the vote and, if any changes that might take place as an outcome would encourage or discourage a return to Poland.

The research was based on a survey circulated to 620 Polish men and women of which 60% were female, and it is the authors' analysis of the surveys which provides the basis for the volume that follows. The respondents chosen were in the main migrants that had been resident in Britain for between ten to twenty years, the majority having arrived post the 2004 accession of Poland to the European Union. They were aged from 20 to late 50s; in low paid to well paid jobs and occupations ranging from blue collar to high level white collar and with English fluency levels varying from excellent to poor. Significantly, as a general rule, the women surveyed proved to be better educated than their male counterparts, having at least one university degree and in well paid professional positions.

Similar to many British citizens, the Polish migrants viewed the forthcoming departure of Britain from the European Union with a degree of scepticism, admitting to being ill-informed regarding both the long and short term implications of Brexit. Despite of their lack of knowledge about what the future might hold, the largest number of the group surveyed were unsure as to whether they would leave Britain and return to Poland. By leaving they would forego the benefits of the pull factors that had drawn them to Britain originally: social security, high wages, and future prospects which would include a pension once British status had been granted. Indeed, a number of those who reported that they were thinking of leaving the United Kingdom had applied for, and had been granted, settled status, thus leaving the door open for a seamless return to the security they had enjoyed.

In contrast to those Polish migrants who valued the benefits of living and working in the United Kingdom and thus remained unsure as to if and when they would return to their home country, there were others who had the positive goal of return at some time in the future, this was seen as confirming the reality rather than the myth of return. Among these were parents concerned about their children's religious upbringing and thus saw Poland, which has an 87% Catholic population, as more suited to maintaining familial religion. There were others that missed their families and family life. Finally, there were those that having seen the Polish economy improve, were now aware of the opportunities that were on offer in their home country.

The detailed accounts of the results of the surveys carried out in the three cities illustrate the different aspects of the Polish migrant community in Britain and their attitude to the possible implications of Brexit; ones which only a minority of respondents tended to discount. Other, more recent, research has shown that the responses revealed in the authors' survey were reflective of the views of the general Polish immigrant population in Britain and, indeed, those of many of the migrants that had settled in the United Kingdom from other European countries following the accessions of 2004 and 2007.[4]

In concluding, it would appear that even though the survey revealed a lack of confidence about if and when the respondents might return home it is perhaps worth noting that, at the time of my writing, UK government statistics reveal that the size of the Polish community is around the 700,00 level, a reduction of at least 300,000 since the beginning of this decade.[5] There is no doubt that some of the Polish migrants have made the decision to leave, what is not known is whether that was due to Brexit, discrimination and exploitation at work – particularly during COVID – or to what they perceived as the opportunity for a more positive and fulfilling life in Poland. Whilst this volume cannot give us an answer it does provide a valuable insight into the thinking of a representative sample of the Polish migrant population in the United Kingdom in 2019 and arguably, whether or not that sample has had a change of heart. This book provides a fascinating lens into the views and thinking of one group of migrant settlers in Britain and as such provides a valuable template for future research of this kind.

Anne J Kershen
QMUL

## Notes

1  Whilst the majority electorate of England and Wales (excluding Greater London) had voted to leave, Scotland and Northern Ireland had voted remain.
2  My research following the Brexit vote revealed that a number of Europeans, including those in the field of medicine and the world of academia, returned home as they felt they didn't want to remain in a country that didn't appear to value their presence.
3  As a point of comparison, the Indian migrant community was the largest group *born* outside of the UK.
4  A recent survey carried out by the University of Middlesex, together with the Universities of Glasgow and Sheffield revealed that at least 33% of the Polish migrant population of Britain had returned home and others were considering it. They blamed Brexit and the fact that the vote had made them feel unwelcome together with unease over the pandemic and a belief they were being discriminated at work and treated unfairly. Mdx.ac.uk/new/2022/10/Brexit-polish – workers; accessed 23 July 2023.
5  Statistics vary as to the exact reduction in numbers.

# Foreword

Our book aims to present the results of quantitative sociological research conducted in Britain in the autumn of 2019 among a sample of Polish migrants living there. The research was motivated by scientific curiosity about the social changes resulting from the outcome of the referendum on the United Kingdom's withdrawal from the European Union. The question we asked ourselves was how Polish people in Britain perceived their further stay there in the context of Brexit and what consequences of Brexit they predicted for their personal, family, and professional life. This book's central point of reference was the dilemma of whether to stay abroad or return to Poland.

Brexit undoubtedly caused many to examine and revise their migration strategy. This means that the change it has brought about may either contribute to their stronger sociocultural embeddedness and integration into the community of the country of settlement or precipitate the decision to return to the country of origin.

The monograph titled *Polish Return Migration after Brexit: A Sociological Forecast* is a sociological study in which we present the attitudes of Polish migrants in the British Isles to the United Kingdom's departure from the European Union. The book consists of chapters, in which we present the results of our research in a multifaceted manner. In the first chapter, we discuss the complexity of the migration phenomenon, present the characteristics of the sample, and describe the method applied in our field research. From the perspective of its research problem, the central part of the monograph is the second chapter, in which we present the results concerning our respondents' perception of Brexit.

The third and fourth chapters present research results concerning the dilemma of whether to stay in the United Kingdom or return to Poland. This dilemma and the respondents' potential decisions seem to be important from the perspectives of both Poland and the United Kingdom. The research results may be helpful in building forecasts and recommendations for those institutions whose activity is based on Polish migrants in the British Isles and for potential employers in their country of origin.

In the third chapter, we analyse the respondents' self-reported motives for remaining in the United Kingdom after Brexit, reflected in the administrative steps they took to make this possible. In this chapter, Polish people's motivations for remaining in the United Kingdom after Brexit are also juxtaposed with their reasons for coming to the United Kingdom which they considered when deciding to emigrate years before.

In the fourth part of the monograph, we present the diversity of return migration trends and attempt to identify the motives that respondents were guided by when deciding to return to Poland. The migrants included in the study were planning to return in the nearest future (within a few years) or in an indefinite future (in more than three years).

We would like to give our thanks to the individuals and institutions whom this book would not have been possible without. Our special gratitude goes to the Rev. Monsignor Stefan Wylężek, Rector of the Polish Catholic Mission in England and Wales, for his fruitful cooperation in the stage of conducting research in Britain and during the writing of this book, which – we hope – will be useful not only to migration sociologists, economists, and demographers but also to social activists, diplomats, entrepreneurs, and clerics ministering among the Poles as a tool for diagnosing the current situation and forecasting the future of Polish cultural and religious centres in the United Kingdom. We also wish to thank the personnel of the Embassy and Consulate of the Republic of Poland in London for their fruitful cooperation in the stages of field research and the dissemination of its results.

Marek Wodawski, Stanisław Fel, and Jarosław Kozak

# I Contemporary Polish Migrants in Britain

## Introduction

The influx of Poles to Britain observed over the last two decades attracts the attention of researchers in many disciplines of social sciences. The contemporary "migration of peoples" is, above all, economic migration. What plays a considerable role in the choice of the United Kingdom as a settlement destination is the geographical and cultural proximity of Western European countries. An additional factor encouraging emigration to the United Kingdom is the belief – still functioning in Polish society – about Western European prosperity. The features that distinguish the latest migration from previous migratory waves include the high dispersion of Polish migrants in Britain. The geography of migratory movements is completely different now than it was a few decades ago, mainly because it is much more unpredictable and irregular (Krotofil, 2013, pp. 15–16).

It is difficult to estimate the scale of the post-accession migration phenomenon. This is caused not only by the lack of precise data concerning the number of migrants arriving and departing but also by the vagueness of the criteria for distinguishing "circular migration" from people returning to Poland permanently. Nevertheless, the United Kingdom, which was among the first countries to open its labour market to citizens of new EU member states, giving them the possibility of legal employment, became the most popular destination for economic migrants at the beginning of the new millennium. It seems that the arrival of so many Poles in Britain had consequences not only in the economic sector and in the results of economic analyses but also in the areas of culture, religion, education, and social relations. Workforce resources enriched by Polish employees resulted in the British economy being capable of developing dynamically, but the unexpected further influx of migrants in subsequent years proved to be a considerable challenge for Britain (Kisiel, Lizińska, & Rosochacka, 2019, p. 134). Only 12 years after the opening of borders for Poles, the British people's decision that the United Kingdom itself would leave the European Union (Brexit) diametrically altered their perception of migrants.

The Brexit referendum, which initiated Britain's withdrawal from the European Union, led to a significant change in migration determinants for the

DOI: 10.4324/9781003449843-1

Poles. The uncertainty about the future fate of Polish citizens in the British Isles induces many of them to consider returning to their homeland. Post-accession migrations were determined mostly by the economic factor. It was the main force motivating potential migrants to change their country of residence and work.

The factors that induce migrants to stay in the country of settlement are:

- the prospect of higher earnings;
- attachment to the family that one is abroad with;
- the length of residence abroad;
- a need for changes in life;
- conviction about the higher standard of living in Western Europe;
- the continuation (or beginning) of children's education in the British school system;
- the global nature of the recession following the COVID-19 pandemic; and
- the war in Ukraine.

As regards returning to the country of origin, the factors inducing migrants to make this decision are:

- the administrative problems that emigrants may encounter after Brexit;
- conviction about the improvement of the economic situation in Poland;
- uncertainty about the availability of social benefits in the United Kingdom after Brexit;
- no command of English (language barriers);
- the "axiological conflict" resulting from the multicultural character of British society;
- separation from the family;
- health problems; and
- nostalgia for the homeland and for the values, customs, and tradition of the country of origin.

## The Nature of Contemporary Migration

Recent years have witnessed a marked increase in the number of Poles living outside their homeland. Poland's accession to the European Union and the opening of the labour markets in 2004 considerably increased the size of the Polish diaspora by adding post-accession migrants to it. The contemporary community of economic migrants includes not only those who hope to return to their home country but also those who want their future to be bound up with permanent residence in the United Kingdom (Kozak, 2015, p. 99). Two distinct phenomena associated with plans of returning to Poland can also be observed increasingly often – namely, return migration and circular migration. That being said, research about migrants is conducted mainly on purposive samples, but – despite their non-representativeness – its results may indicate the existence of certain phenomena, strategies, and problems in the population as a whole (Iglicka, 2010, p. 23). Another phenomenon, much smaller in scale, is transit migration. The term covers all people who migrate across multiple countries. So far, transit migration has been relatively easy thanks to the freedom of movement, for example between the countries of the European Union. Brexit may, though it does not have to, increase migrations between European countries – i.e., further movement not just to the home country but to other EU countries as well. It can therefore be predicted that the Poles living in Britain will also look for other European countries of settlement as the destinations of their migration.

In the light of what has been discussed here, it seems legitimate to conduct sociological research into the attitudes towards Brexit found among Polish people, both among those planning to stay in the United Kingdom and among those planning to return to Poland. Their dilemmas may intensify due to the COVID-19 pandemic, which, since the early months of 2020, has affected all spheres of human existence on a global scale, and the ongoing war in Ukraine, which directly borders on Poland.

## The Research Problem of this Monograph

The research problem investigated in our study is Polish migrants' attitudes towards Brexit and their decisions dictated by the socioeconomic changes Brexit is causing. To better explain the patterns that we have found during our research, we will attempt to answer the following questions.

- What is the level of interest in Brexit issues among Polish migrants in Britain?
- What is their evaluation of how Brexit-related information is communicated by Polish and British authorities?
- What is the impact of Polish and British mass media on their knowledge about Brexit?
- What is their evaluation of Britain's preparations for leaving the European Union?
- How did they feel about the referendum campaign that preceded Brexit?
- Do they perceive Brexit as a gain or loss for Poland, Britain, and the European Union as a whole?
- What, in their opinion, are the downsides and benefits of Brexit?
- What are their predictions regarding the dynamics of the ongoing process of the United Kingdom's departure from the European Union?

Additionally, for the purpose of comparative analysis, we were interested in the following issues:

- What were Polish migrants' main reasons for deciding to come to Britain and what and what are their main arguments for returning to Poland?
- What time of returning to Poland do they consider?
- How do respondents identify their nationality?
- Have they experienced discrimination in Britain before or after the Brexit referendum?
- What are their possible reasons for staying in Britain after Brexit?
- Have they taken administrative steps to guarantee their further stay in the United Kingdom after Brexit?
- What is their evaluation of their engagement in the activities of Polish community organisations in Britain so far and what is their opinion on whether Brexit can change the degree or type of this engagement?

## Sample and Procedure

The sociological research included Poles living in three English cities, which differed in terms of size and character. In this research project, in October 2019, we surveyed 620 adults – 189 respondents in London, 198 in Oxford, and 233 in Swindon. The three cities surveyed are characterised by different urbanisation structures, living conditions, living standards, and the nature of the professional work undertaken by expatriates from Poland. London is undoubtedly the most diverse in many respects in terms of the concentration of the so-called old and new Polonia; here almost everyone can find work in their profession. The situation for Poles in Oxford, a small city of only 155,000 inhabitants, is different. Here, Poles not only work in low-skilled services, but also find employment in academic positions and in the administration of the two large universities and in reputable hospitals. Swindon, on the other hand, is a typical industrial town with over 20% more inhabitants than Oxford. It is also one of the largest concentrations of Poles in England. There are various Polish migrant communities, a Polish Catholic parish, Polish Saturday schools, pubs, restaurants, etc. in this town. The sampling was purposive. Expert (purposive) samples have already been successfully used in social sciences in empirical studies whose aims included the forecasting of changes on many planes of the social structure (Kozak, 2015, p. 106). It is on this particular type of samples that sociological studies involving return migrants are very often conducted; the analysis of the overall data collected as a result of this kind of quantitative research allows for identifying the trends present in the population.

The survey questionnaire used in the field research in Britain was anonymous and consisted of 35 closed-ended questions focused on the knowledge and opinions of the Poles living there about Brexit. It also included questions about their reasons for coming to the British Isles, their plans of returning to Poland or remaining in the United Kingdom, and their reasons for making these plans. Some of the questions focused on self-reported national identity, engagement in Polish community organisations, and any instances of discrimination due to nationality experienced in Britain. The study was conducted using the auditorium questionnaire technique. Avoiding the distributed questionnaire method, we achieved a nearly 100 percent return rate (Kauf & Tłuczak, 2013, p. 28). We conducted our research in locations with the largest Polish communities in the United Kingdom, including Polish schools and parishes run by the Polish Catholic Mission in England and Wales.

## Respondents' Sociodemographic Characteristics

Emigration is an immensely interesting research area, encompassing nearly all dimensions of human existence, which makes it a difficult challenge for scholars doing quantitative research. The difficulty lies in reaching the respondents and, above all, in relating the collected data to the rapidly changing reality. When analysing the research problem, we sought to capture a long-term perspective in the respondents' perception of the Brexit situation, including their plans associated with permanent settlement in or departure from the United Kingdom. Bearing in mind the different variants of how the European Union versus Britain scenario might develop and the related circumstances directly influencing the attitudes of the Poles in Britain, one should be aware of the possible need to revise the interpretation of the phenomena under discussion. Two months after the completion of quantitative research, when Big Ben was announcing the United Kingdom's departure from the European Union to the world, in a different part of the globe a pandemic was brewing that would soon reach Europe and become a worldwide issue. Therefore, rather than provide a complete picture of Polish migrants in the United Kingdom, the results of the analyses presented below constitute a small step towards the understanding of the Brexit-induced sociopolitical changes taking place in the Polish diaspora.

Among the many demographic and social characteristics of the examined population of Polish expatriates, there are a few that deserve special attention in further statistical analyses. In the present text, we discuss the demographic and social characteristics included in the respondent's particular section of the survey questionnaire. Some of them are treated as independent variables. They will provide a clue about the directions of possible changes in the attitudes of Polish expatriates. Against the backdrop of the emerging opinions and views on the rapid sociopolitical changes in Britain, extensive sociological research into migrants' attitudes towards these changes will make it possible to verify the widespread conjectures, judgements, and even stereotypes regarding the situation in which Britain and, more broadly, the entire European Union have found themselves.

When studying Polish migrants who arrived in Britain in recent years, one observes that, despite a certain range of common experience, there is considerable diversity within this group, resulting from their migration strategies and settlement plans and from the degree of commitment to integration and assimilation. The clearly visible phenomenon of some groups of migrants in Britain creating easily recognisable communities, usually located in a specific space, stems from an attempt to overcome the limitations that may be attributable to the immigrant status (Krotofil, 2013, p. 18).

As mentioned before, among the many different demographic and social characteristics of Poles in Britain, there are several that deserve special attention in subsequent statistical analyses. Some of them will be treated in further analyses as independent variables: gender, age, education, occupation type, financial situation, command of English, the level of engagement in Polish community organisations in Britain, and the length of residence abroad. Regarding age categories, in the analyses we divided the migrants into groups under the age of 30, in their 30s, in their 40s, and aged 50 or above. This means that the respondents in the first two categories can be classified as being in the mobile productive age, whereas the other two are workers approaching or entering the non-mobile productive age (Murkowski, 2011, p. 441). Respondents' education was categorised as follows: primary or basic vocational education were recoded as one variable; secondary education was understood as general secondary, technical secondary, or post-secondary; finally, higher education was divided into two categories: higher vocational (bachelor's degree) and higher (master's degree). Current occupation type took the form of blue-collar or white-collar worker categories in further statistical analyses. Respondents' financial situation was categorised as definitely good or fairly good. Because none of the respondents defined their financial situation as definitely poor, "average" and "rather poor" responses were treated as falling into one category. Command of English was categorized in our study as very good, good, and basic conversational, plus one category covering self-reported poor, very poor, or no command of English. Specific categories of engagement in the activity of Polish community organisations in Britain were based on the five-point Likert scale used in the survey questionnaire, with one meaning no engagement and five indicating a high level of engagement. In further analyses, these values were recoded as follows: engaged – the first two responses; moderately engaged – the medium value on the scale; non-engaged – the last two options on the response scale. For length of residence abroad, there were three categories: up to ten years (arrived in Britain between 2010 and 2019), 10–20 years (arrived between 2000 and 2009), and more than 20 years' residence (arrived before 2000).

*a) Respondents' Gender*

The subjects were 218 men, who accounted for 35.2% of the sample, and 388 women, (62.6%). Of the respondents, 14 (2.2%) did not report their gender in the survey questionnaire (Table 1.1).

Men turned out to be more willing to return to their country of origin than to remain in Britain. Every third man had no specific plans on whether to

*Table 1.1* Respondents' gender and self-reported intention to return to Poland

| Categories of answers | Within a few years | | In an indefinite future | | Never | | Hard to say | |
|---|---|---|---|---|---|---|---|---|
| | N | % | N | % | N | % | N | % |
| Male | 59 | 41 | 69 | 37.1 | 23 | 26.4 | 67 | 33 |
| Female | 81 | 56.3 | 114 | 61.3 | 62 | 71.3 | 131 | 64.5 |
| Not reported | 4 | 2.8 | 3 | 1.6 | 2 | 2.3 | 5 | 2.5 |
| Total | 144 | 100 | 186 | 100 | 87 | 100 | 203 | 100 |

return or to stay. In other words, men were dominant among returnees, while women were dominant among those preferred to stay; there was also a trend indicating considerably more women undecided about returning or staying.

The highest proportion of men belonged to the group of respondents in their 30s (41.8%). A substantial majority of men had primary or basic vocational education (68.8%) and worked in occupations that required physical activity (65.2%). Men most often reported a fairly good financial situation (44.3%) and a good command of English (35.5%). Two in three men (62.4%) had lived abroad for 10–20 years.

As in the case of the men, the largest number of women in the group were aged 30–39 years (46.2%). Women most often had higher education (45.6%), worked in occupations requiring intellectual activity (57.1%), reported a good financial situation (48.6%), and had a very good command of English (40.9%), which means they used the language of their country of settlement better than the men. As in the group of men, also in the female group the largest number of migrants had lived in Britain for 10–20 years (63.4%).

### b) Respondents' Age

In the examined population, four in ten respondents were in their 30s (30–39 years – 42.6%), nearly one in three was in their 40s (40–49 years – 30.8%), one in ten was over 50 (≥50 years – 10.6%), and one in nine was 29 or younger at the time of the study (11%) (Table 1.2).

In the group of migrants in their 30s, nearly every second respondent had not yet made their decision to stay in Britain or return to Poland, four in ten reported an intention to return to Poland, and one in three reported an intention to remain in England permanently.

Among the respondents under the age of 30, 61.8% were women and 38.2% were men. This age group most often reported general secondary, technical secondary, or post-secondary education (38.2%). The youngest respondents were more often white-collar workers than blue-collar ones (52.6% versus 47.4%) and reported a fairly good financial situation (46.9%). Every second

*Table 1.2* Respondents' age and self-reported intention to return to Poland

| Categories of answers | Within a few years | | In an indefinite future | | Never | | Hard to say | |
|---|---|---|---|---|---|---|---|---|
| | N | % | N | % | N | % | N | % |
| <30 | 19 | 13.2 | 18 | 9.7 | 14 | 16.1 | 17 | 8.4 |
| 30–39 | 59 | 41 | 77 | 41.4 | 32 | 36.8 | 96 | 47.3 |
| 40–49 | 40 | 27.8 | 64 | 34.4 | 24 | 27.6 | 63 | 31 |
| ≥50 | 18 | 12.5 | 20 | 10.8 | 12 | 13.8 | 16 | 7.9 |
| Total | 136 | 100 | 179 | 100 | 82 | 100 | 192 | 100 |

respondent in this age group had a very good command of the language of the country of settlement (48.5%). The vast majority of the youngest respondents (73.1%) had lived in Britain for less than ten years.

The group in their 30s was also predominantly female (M = 38.2%, W = 61.8%). These respondents more often reported having a master's degree (36.9%) or secondary education (35.7%). They more often worked in occupations that required physical activity (53.8%), reported a fairly good financial situation (39.9%), and had a very good or good command of English (37.3%). Migrants in their 30s had usually already begun their second decade of residence in Britain (10–20 years – 67.8%).

Women were dominant among the expatriates in their 40s as well (M = 36.1%, W = 63.9%). In this age group, respondents most often had higher education (master's degree; 51.1%), did white-collar jobs (57.1%), reported a fairly good financial situation (46.6%), and had a good or very good command of English (36.8% and 36.3%, respectively). Three out of four expatriates in their 40s had lived in Britain for 10–20 years (72.1%), and one in five had lived there for less than ten years (21.6%).

In the case of the oldest respondents, aged 50 or above at the time of the study, women were found to be more numerous than men, too (60.6%). The oldest expatriates most often had secondary education (40.9%), considerably more often worked in occupations involving physical activity (73.1%), and reported a fairly good financial situation (50%). They evaluated their English as basic conversational (30.8%) or admitted that their command of that language was poor or none (27.7%). Like other age groups, the oldest respondents had most often lived abroad for 10–20 years (57.1%).

### c) Respondents' Education

In the analysed sample, nearly four in ten respondents had higher education (master's degree – 37.7%), one in three had secondary education (general secondary, technical secondary, or post-secondary – 33.7%), one in five had higher vocational education (bachelor's degree – 19%), and one in thirteen had primary or basic vocational education (7.7%). Eleven respondents (1.8%) did not answer the question about education at all. According to data from our sociological survey, almost all of them graduated in Poland (Table 1.3).

Those who had not yet decided whether to stay or return usually had higher education (bachelor's or master's degree). Expatriates reporting an intention to return to Poland in the nearest future tended to have general secondary, technical secondary, or post-secondary education. Higher vocational education (bachelor's degree) was indicated by every fifth respondent reporting an intention to return to Poland soon or to remain in Britain permanently (19.5%). The migrants with a master's degree included nearly every second woman (45.6%) and every fourth man (25.3%), every second respondent in his or her 40s (50.8%), every third migrant in the oldest group in our sociological study (≥50 years – 33.3%), and three times more white-collar workers than blue-collar ones (59.9% versus 18.8%). The group included 45.5% of those who regarded their financial situation as definitely good. The best-educated group was also the one with the highest proportion of individuals reporting a very good command of English (52.2%). Four out of ten respondents engaged in Polish community organisations (43.4%), a somewhat lower percentage of non-engaged respondents (38.6%), and every third moderately engaged one (32.2%) belonged to this group.

Among those who had primary or basic vocational education, there were two times more men than women (68.8% versus 31.3%). The largest number of respondents in this group were in their 30s (30.4%) and 40s (26.1%). A large disproportion was found between occupation type categories (blue-collar workers – 85.7%, white-collar workers – 14.3%). Respondents with the lowest education evaluated their financial situation as fairly good (40.9%) or as average or rather poor (38.6%). They most often reported a basic conversational (39.6%) or poor (20.8%) command of English. Most of them (61.7%) had been expatriates for 10–20 years.

Respondents reporting general secondary, technical secondary, or post-secondary education were more often women (M = 43.2%, W = 56.8%), individuals in their 30s (47.7%), and people working in occupations requiring physical activity (76%). They usually reported a fairly good or average/poor financial situation (48.9% versus 39.5%, respectively) and a good command of English (40.9%). The majority of these migrants had begun their second decade of residence abroad (10–20 years – 61.8%).

Respondents with higher vocational education were also more frequently women (M = 33.9%, W = 66.1%), people in their 30s (50%), white-collar workers (53.8%), migrants reporting a fairly good financial situation (43.9%), and ones with a very good command of English (43.2%). These respondents had usually lived abroad for 10–20 years (65.2%).

The respondents in the best-educated group were much more frequently women than men (M = 23.8%, W = 76.2%), predominantly people in their

*Table 1.3* Respondents' education and self-reported intention to return to Poland

| Categories of answers | Within a few years | | In an indefinite future | | Never | | Hard to say | |
|---|---|---|---|---|---|---|---|---|
| | N | % | N | % | N | % | N | % |
| Primary or basic vocational | 7 | 4.9 | 22 | 11.8 | 3 | 3.4 | 16 | 7.9 |
| General secondary, technical secondary, or post-secondary | 54 | 37.5 | 66 | 35.5 | 30 | 34.5 | 59 | 29.1 |
| Higher vocational (bachelor's degree) | 31 | 21.5 | 32 | 17.2 | 17 | 19.5 | 38 | 18.7 |
| Higher (master's degree) | 50 | 34.7 | 64 | 34.4 | 35 | 40.2 | 85 | 41.9 |
| Not reported | 2 | 1.4 | 2 | 1.1 | 2 | 2.3 | 5 | 2.5 |
| Total | 144 | 100 | 186 | 100 | 87 | 100 | 203 | 100 |

30s or 40s (42.2% in both cases), white-collar workers (75.2%), and – as in the previously discussed group – individuals reporting a fairly good financial situation (48.9%). They were the best users of English, too (very good command – 50.4%, good command – 32.1%). Like the remaining respondents, migrants with a master's degree had most often lived abroad for 10–20 years.

### d) Respondents' Occupation Type

The group of blue-collar workers included two-thirds of self-employed respondents (64%), nearly every second employee (47.8%), and one in three entrepreneurs (33.3%). This means that every third self-employed respondent (36%), every second employee (52.2%), and two in three entrepreneurs were white-collar workers (66.7%) (Table 1.4).

The group of blue-collar workers included a considerable majority of respondents reporting an intention to return to the country of origin, nearly every second undecided respondent, and every third migrant planning to remain in Britain permanently. Consequently, the majority of respondents who had decided not to return to Poland, more than half of the undecided ones, and considerably fewer of those reporting an intention to return (in an indefinite future – 45.6%, within a few years – 37.6%) were white-collar workers.

In the group of blue-collar workers, we found comparable percentages of men and women (M = 47.7%, W = 52.6%). The most numerous among them were respondents in their 30s (48.6%), with secondary general, secondary technical, or post-secondary education (51.7%), and in a fairly good financial situation (47.1%), though in this group we also found a high percentage of individuals reporting average or rather poor financial situation (42.2%). Blue-collar workers reported a good command of English (41.5%). Most of them (61.6%) had lived abroad for 10–20 years.

White-collar workers were mostly women (M = 26.5%, K = 73.5%), respondents in their 30s (43.9%) or 40s (39.4%) and usually with a master's degree (59.9%). They evaluated their financial situation as fairly good (48.8%) and reported a very good command of English (59.5%). Respondents who had been expatriates for 10–20 years constituted 65.7% of this group.

### e) Respondents' Financial Situation

At the time of the study, nearly four in ten respondents reported a fairly good financial situation (42.9%), one in three reported average or rather poor financial situation (34%), every seventh respondent rated theirs as very good (14.2%), and every eleventh refused to answer this question (8.9%) (Table 1.5).

A fairly good financial situation was reported by every second respondent planning to remain in Britain permanently (51.7%) and every second one

*Table 1.4* Respondents' occupation type and self-reported intention to return to Poland

| Categories of answers | Within a few years | | In an indefinite future | | Never | | Hard to say | |
|---|---|---|---|---|---|---|---|---|
| | N | % | N | % | N | % | N | % |
| Blue-collar worker | 83 | 62.4 | 93 | 54.4 | 26 | 35.6 | 86 | 46.5 |
| White-collar worker | 50 | 37.6 | 78 | 45.6 | 47 | 64.4 | 99 | 53.5 |
| Total | 133 | 100 | 171 | 100 | 73 | 100 | 185 | 100 |

*Table 1.5* Respondents' financial situation and self-reported intention to return to Poland

| Categories of answers | Within a few years | | In an indefinite future | | Never | | Hard to say | |
|---|---|---|---|---|---|---|---|---|
| | N | % | N | % | N | % | N | % |
| Definitely good | 27 | 18.8 | 21 | 11.3 | 18 | 20.7 | 22 | 10.8 |
| Fairly good | 50 | 34.7 | 70 | 37.6 | 45 | 51.7 | 101 | 49.8 |
| Average or rather poor | 50 | 34.7 | 79 | 42.5 | 16 | 18.4 | 66 | 32.5 |
| Not reported | 17 | 11.8 | 16 | 8.6 | 8 | 9.2 | 14 | 6.9 |
| Total | 144 | 100 | 186 | 100 | 87 | 100 | 203 | 100 |

undecided about returning or staying abroad (49.8%). Four in ten migrants planning to return from abroad in an indefinite future (42.5%) evaluated their financial situation as average or rather poor. A definitely good financial situation could be observed in the case of every fifth respondent who intended to stay in England permanently (20.7%) and slightly less often among those planning to return to Poland as soon as possible (18.8%).

A definitely good financial situation was most often reported by women (M = 41.9%, W = 58.1%), respondents in their 30s (43.5%), best-educated ones (with master's degrees – 46%), white-collar workers (66.3%), very good users of English (58.6%), and respondents who had lived abroad for 10–20 years (67.1%).

The group reporting a fairly good financial situation was also dominated by women (67.2%), respondents in their 30s (44.7%), and individuals with master's degrees (40.5%) or secondary education (35.2%). The group included similar proportions of blue-collar and white-collar workers (50.4% versus 49.6%, respectively). These respondents most often had a very good (39%) or good (38.3%) command of English. As regards the length of residence in Britain, migrants who had begun their second decade of expatriate life were in the majority in this group as well (10–20 years' residence – 64.9%).

The worst financial situation was reported by one in three men and by two in three women (M = 34.6%, W = 65.4%), most often in their 30s (45%), with general secondary, technical secondary, or post-secondary education (36.1%) or (master's degree, 34.6%), blue-collar workers (60.3%), with good (33.2%) or basic conversational English (29.3%). This group consisted predominantly of individuals who had lived abroad for 10–20 years.

### f) Respondents' Command of English

In the analysed research sample, 36.5% of respondents reported a very good command of English, nearly every third respondent considered their command of English good (34%), and one in five rated theirs as basic conversational (21.6%). Only 6.3% indicated that their command of the language of the country of settlement was poor or that they did not use it at all. Ten respondents did not answer the question about their command of English (1.6%) (Table 1.6).

Nearly two in three respondents planning to remain permanently in Britain reported very good English (62.1%). A very good command of the language spoken in their country of settlement was reported by almost four in ten migrants undecided about their further stay in the British Isles (38.4%), every third respondent planning to return to Poland (in an indefinite future – 35.5%, within a few years – 35.4%), and nearly every second respondent intending to remain in Britain permanently (18.4%). Individuals with basic conversational English were most numerous among the respondents who reported an intention to return to Poland (within a few years – 29.2%, in an indefinite future

*Table 1.6* Respondents' command of English and self-reported intention to return to Poland

| | Within a few years | | In an indefinite future | | Never | | Hard to say | |
|---|---|---|---|---|---|---|---|---|
| | N | % | N | % | N | % | N | % |
| Very good | 38 | 26.4 | 59 | 31.7 | 54 | 62.1 | 75 | 36.9 |
| Good | 51 | 35.4 | 66 | 35.5 | 16 | 18.4 | 78 | 38.4 |
| Basic conversational | 42 | 29.2 | 43 | 23.1 | 12 | 13.8 | 37 | 18.2 |
| Poor or none | 11 | 7.6 | 15 | 8.1 | 3 | 3.4 | 10 | 4.9 |
| Not reported | 2 | 1.4 | 3 | 1.6 | 2 | 2.3 | 3 | 1.5 |
| Total | 144 | 100 | 186 | 100 | 87 | 100 | 203 | 100 |

– 23.1%). A poor command or no command of English was almost two times more frequent among respondents who intended to return to Poland (in an indefinite future – 8.1%; within a few years – 7.6%) than among undecided ones (4.9%) or among those who planned to remain in the United Kingdom (3.4%).

A good command of English was reported by 63.3% of women and nearly two times fewer men (36.7%); the largest number of these respondents were in their 30s (47.6%), had secondary education (45.1%), and worked in occupations requiring physical rather than intellectual activity (58.3% versus 41.7%, respectively). The highest proportion of respondents with a good command of English were found among those who evaluated their financial situation as fairly good (51.8%) and among those who had lived as expatriates for 10–20 years (53.1%) or for less than ten years (45.3%).

Command of English was basic conversational in slightly more women than men (M = 45.54%, W = 54.5%), mostly among respondents in their 30s (41%), with secondary education (45.1%), doing blue-collar jobs (79.5%), reporting an average or rather poor financial situation (50.4%), with 10–20 years of residence abroad behind them (53.1%).

In the group with a poor command or no command of the language used in the country of settlement, the most numerous respondents were also women (M = 41%, W = 59%), the oldest migrants aged over 50 (46.2%), with secondary education (43.6%) or with primary or basic vocational education (25.6%), blue-collar workers (93.5%), mostly reporting an average or rather poor financial situation (68.6%). The majority of this group were individuals who had lived abroad for less than ten years (54.1%).

### g) Respondents' Length of Residence in the United Kingdom

In the population surveyed, we found twice as many individuals had arrived in Britain in the years 2000–2009 (60.8%) than those who had arrived in 2010 or later (32.3%). The smallest group were respondents who had come to Britain before 2000 (3.4%), and the proportion of those who gave no answer to this question was 3.5%. During empirical analysis concerning the length of respondents' residence in Britain, and when recoding this variable into three categories using SPSS, we decided to exclude systematic missing data from further analysis. As a result, the percentage of migrants who had lived in the United Kingdom for 10–20 years was 63%, 33.4% had been there for less than ten years, and those with the longest expatriate life behind them – more than 20 years – accounted for 3.5% (Table 1.7).

The respondents who had started their second decade away from the country of origin were characterised by uncertainty about whether to remain in the United Kingdom or return to Poland. The group of migrants whose length of residence abroad did not exceed ten years included nearly every second respondent reporting an intention to return to Poland within a few years.

*Table 1.7* Length of residence in the United Kingdom and self-reported intention to return to Poland

| Categories of answers | Within a few years | | In an indefinite future | | Never | | Hard to say | |
|---|---|---|---|---|---|---|---|---|
| | N | % | N | % | N | % | N | % |
| <10 years (arrived 2010–2019) | 67 | 47.5 | 63 | 35.2 | 22 | 26.5 | 48 | 24.6 |
| 10–20 years (arrived 2000–2009) | 72 | 51.1 | 112 | 62.6 | 52 | 62.7 | 141 | 72.3 |
| >20 years (arrived before 2000) | 2 | 1.4 | 4 | 2.2 | 9 | 10.8 | 6 | 3.1 |
| Total | 141 | 100 | 179 | 100 | 83 | 100 | 195 | 100 |

Those who had lived in the United Kingdom the longest included every ninth migrant who intended to stay in Britain permanently.

The migrants who had lived in Britain for the shortest time (less than ten years) were predominantly women (M = 34.7%, W = 65.3%), respondents in their 30s (43.3%), well-educated people (master's degree – 38.2%), blue-collar workers (56.4%), individuals rating their financial situation as fairly good (45.7%), and respondents with a good command of English (33.7%).

The group of respondents who had lived in Britain for 10–20 years by the time of the study was also characterised by a predominance of women (M = 35.4%, W = 64.6%), migrants in their 30s (48.5%), and people with a higher education (master's degree, 38.7%), and included comparable proportions of white-collar (50.1%) and blue-collar workers (49.9%). Migrants in this group most often reported a fairly good financial situation (48%) and a very good command of English (40.5%).

Those with the longest time of residence in Britain behind them (more than 20 years) were slightly more often men (M = 52.4%, W = 47.6%), individuals in their 40s (57.1%) or over the age of 50 (33.3%), and those reporting secondary education (42.9%) or a master's degree (38.1%). This group was predominantly composed of white-collar workers (70.6%) and respondents in a fairly good financial situation (41.2%) reporting a very good command of English (66.7%).

## Summary

The analysis of the surveyed sample of Polish migrants in the United Kingdom leads to several conclusions. What emerges from the presented research results is a picture of a relatively young migrant in a forced situation of suspension between staying and returning. Even though there is no necessity for the migrants to clearly decide between life in the country of origin and life in the country of settlement, Brexit is undoubtedly a source of their internal frustration. This is not a case of bitterness being understood as nostalgia for the country of origin, or a matter of deficits perceived in the migration situation, such as the absence of family; this is a matter of uncertainty about the very conditions of further life abroad outside the European Union. Post-accession migration is of a different nature to earlier migration waves, such as those known from post-war history. The economic factors stimulating emigration, especially among young people, during the first years after EU accession, may have led to a form of desperation pushing the Poles abroad. This desperation was additionally increased by the economic crisis in Poland, high unemployment, and no prospects of career development. Currently, Polish migrants living in Britain consider their decisions to return to their homeland or remain outside the European Union in conjunction with other factors, including religious and cultural ones, which will be discussed further in this monograph.

# References

Iglicka, Krystyna. (2010). *Powroty Polaków po 2004 roku: w pętli pułapki migracji.* Warszawa: Wydawnictwo Naukowe Scholar.

Kauf, Sabina, & Tłuczak, Agnieszka. (2013). *Metody i techniki badań ankietowych na przykładzie zachowań komunikacyjnych opolan.* Opole: Wydawnictwo Uniwersytetu Opolskiego. https://www.researchgate.net/publication/324731715_Metody_i_techniki_badan_ankietowych_na_przykladzie_zachowan_komunikacyjnych_opolan (2023-01-06)

Kisiel, Roman, Lizińska, Wiesława, & Rosochacka, Paulina. (2019). Migracje zarobkowe Polaków w kontekście brexitu: Gainful Migrations of Poles in the Context of Brexit. *Przegląd Wschodnioeuropejski,* 10 (1), 129–137. https://www.ceeol.com/search/viewpdf?id=804619 (2023-01-06)

Kozak, Jarosław. (2015). *Małżeństwo i rodzina w świadomości nupturientów w Polsce i Wielkiej Brytanii. Studium Socjologiczne na 120-lecie Polskiej Misji Katolickiej Anglii i Walii.* Lublin: Wydawnictwo Gaudium. https://repozytorium.kul.pl/bitstream/20.500.12153/2017/4/Kozak_Jaroslaw_Malzennstwo_i_rodzina.pdf (2023-02-06)

Krotofil, Joanna. (2013). *Religia w procesie kształtowania tożsamości wśród polskich migrantów w Wielkiej Brytanii.* Kraków: Nomos.

Murkowski, Radosław. (2011). Ocena obciążenia demograficznego ludności Polski na lata 2010–2025. *Prace i Materiały Wydziału Zarządzania Uniwersytetu Gdańskiego,* 8 (4), 435–452.

# II Respondents' Evaluation of Brexit and its Effects

## Introduction

One of the most important challenges faced by contemporary society is to ensure the widest possible access to information, since the development of society is undoubtedly promoted by unfettered discourse and free communication between individuals. It is thanks to the flow of information and the social communication institutions that individuals develop rational opinions or even rational will. The information acquired and, consequently, the opinions formed on its basis are significant for the choices individuals make. It should be stressed that there is no automatic relationship between the amount of information acquired, especially detailed information, and the views held or the emotions experienced and the subsequent impact on communal attitudes and actions. In this part of our study, we will analyse respondents' perception of Brexit in the context of media coverage concerning Britain's withdrawal from the European Union.

## The Power of Mass Media in Knowledge Transfer and Opinion Building

In a Eurobarometer survey conducted for the European Commission in 2018, the United Kingdom ranked among the three member states whose citizens' level of knowledge about the European Parliament turned out to be the lowest. When asked a detailed question about the manner of electing Members of the European Parliament, 51% of British citizens gave the correct answer and 24% gave an incorrect one. Every fourth British citizen (25%) chose the "hard to say" response. As regards the Poles, it turned out that the majority answered correctly (70%), only 16% gave a wrong answer, and slightly fewer gave none (14%). When asked what feelings the European Union evoked in them, British respondents usually indicated a positive (43%) or neutral (29%), rather than negative (27%), nature. Polish people answered the same question slightly more enthusiastically (feelings about the European Union: positive – 54%, neutral – 36%, negative – 10%) (Eurobarometer, 2018, pp. 3–5).

DOI: 10.4324/9781003449843-2

The opinion built is not always lasting. Changes in discourse on crucial issues can take place relatively quickly.

> Although, in principle, it is worth popularizing knowledge on the functioning of and dilemmas faced by the European Union, it cannot be assumed that such actions will translate into a change in the attitudes and emotions associated with political discourse in society as a whole and in large social groups.
>
> (Fedorowicz & Skipietrow, 2017, p. 1)

What therefore appears to be a contentious issue is the question about the blurred line that could help establish the extent to which the sum of individuals' opinions makes up public opinion, which seems to be a product of mutual influences between social groups, creating sets of patterns of opposing views and positions on specific issues. This perspective points to the currently common tendency to treat public opinion not as the simple sum of individual opinions but as the sum of relationships between them – as the outcome of different attitudes and views clashing. A characteristic feature of public opinion is the fact that it concerns mostly social needs in the macro space – the issues where the interests of the entire society meet and intersect.

Insofar as every society is characterised by spatial distribution, it is also marked by a certain noticeable and explorable closeness between people that has come into being precisely thanks to the exchange of information, opinions, and suggestions (Tarde, 1904, pp. 36–37). Efficient communication channels enable the natural flow of information stemming from the dynamics of social needs and processes. Providing information, learning, and understanding the needs of society, discussing important social issues, identifying the common interest, and building a consensus and social balance – these are the primary aims of dialogue in society. An ideal communication situation is one that meets the following conditions:

- truth – the communication is true;
- rightness – the communication is consistent with norms regarded as right;
- truthfulness – the communication is in agreement with thought (Misztal, 2015, pp. 119–123).

In the communication of information thus defined, the decisive factor is the presence of the information culture phenomenon, understood in terms of high quality of information transfer, including source data, and the ability to communicate information in a clear and matter-of-fact way, to use the available information resources, to use information in the individual decision-making process, and to learn by linking information from different sources or even from different areas of knowledge. The information culture phenomenon is an evident way of developing opinions based on the available sources of information, by filtering, organizing, selecting, and making use of these sources and thus creating a basis for acquired knowledge. Information culture also includes individual information awareness, thanks to which a person is able to develop new norms, values, attitudes, behaviour patterns, and ways of perceiving information. Information culture should be part of opinion building. An informed citizen in the information society, who has high information culture, actively participates in community life, building a professional information platform (Babik, 2012, p. 33).

The following features of a person's information culture are currently distinguished.

- information integrity, defined as a transparent and trustworthy way of using information on the individual or organisational levels, which has been recognised as individually and socially acceptable information activity;
- information formality, understood as the preference for formalised and therefore reliable sources over informal and frequently unverified information;
- information control, which means constantly verifying the quality of information;
- information transparency, defined as voluntary public provision of information about mistakes and failures so that others can draw conclusions from them;
- information sharing, being the ability and willingness to motivate others to share their ideas and to exchange and share information;
- proactiveness, which consists of creatively using and sharing information and in developing information management and communication practices in response to the demands of the environment (Marchand, Kettinger, & Rollins, 2002, pp. 200–201).

Agnieszka Szymańska believes that, while the transfer of many goods associated with the economic sphere of European integration, such as capital, commodities, and services, or workforce, has been very efficient in the European Union for many years despite the problems that the community's economy is going through, it is still hardly possible to speak of a similarly efficient exchange of political information in the media in its territory. Perhaps this sphere is strictly linked with language as the carrier component of national cultures that constitutes a more effective barrier than culture alone and the model of entrepreneurship functioning in a given society (Szymańska, 2016, p. 41).

On the one hand, information transfer and, consequently, knowledge acquisition and opinion building can strengthen society; on the other, they enable the observation and surveillance of society, which means it is possible to use them to manipulate information both by restricting and by ensuring access to it. Jürgen Habermas advances the thesis that, at present, governments and economic entities attach great importance to information that is reliable and useful to them, but citizens have fewer and fewer opportunities to use public information and express their opinions in an open forum. In the sphere of information transfer we often encounter a reality of ritual chaos, fake discourse, or defiance of the declared normative principles, such as the principle of openness (Habermas, 1989, pp. 5–9). This diagnosis indicates that the contemporary controlled transfer of information tends to serve the purpose of blocking communication and that the recipient – the public sphere – becomes a hoax. The German sociologist observes that the administrative structures of the state are currently becoming the authority that sets the laws, while society only expects these laws to be presented and justified. Public opinion is thus subject to manipulation – people's opinions are probed, and on their basis a picture of a given problem, issue, or reality is built further in the individual's mind (Habermas, 1989, pp. 218–245; Hułas, 2019). "This is a kind of illusion of social control, because thanks to the channels of information transfer the citizen is moulded rather than treated as an equal co-decision-maker" (Ochman, 2015, p. 150).

In communication, a big danger for objective opinion building can be seen, consisting of the risk that, with a simplified one-stage opinion building, recipients may develop a distorted picture of reality. The author of a message is never fully objective, and behind message contents there is always an intention of influencing the recipient. What this amounts to is the idea of imitation – not so much the imitation of behaviours as the imitation and copying of opinions, which then make up the backdrop for the recipient's consciousness (Tarde, 1904, p. 304). Specific opinions, however, would not arise without at least a minimum of intellectual reflection and, prior to that, a minimal interest in the problem, as otherwise the critical reflection factor would also be eliminated from the opinion-building process (Dejneka, 2019, pp. 91–92).

## Polish People's Interest in Political Issues

Since the beginning of the political transformation in 1989, the Public Opinion Research Centre (CBOS – Centrum Badania Opinii Społecznej) has regularly asked Polish people to what extent they are interested in politics. Survey results show that respondents' interest in this domain is small and tends to be relatively stable. In 1990, 17% of respondents reported that they were interested in politics to a high or very high degree, while 36% were interested in it to a slight degree or not interested at all. In the subsequent years, interest in political life diminished. This downward trend continued until 1994, when people interested in politics (to a high or very high degree) accounted for 10% of the population, whereas those with a slight or no interest in it accounted for 48%. In the years 1996–2005, there was no significant change in Polish people's interest in political life: 13%–15% of respondents followed political events fairly attentively, while 38%–43% were only slightly interested in politics or not interested in it at all. After 2006, the percentage of people moderately interested in politics decreased (from 46% in 2006 to 39% in 2009), while the percentage of those who were generally not interested in politics increased (from 39% in 2006 to 49% in 2009). The decrease in Polish people's interest in political issues continued until 2009. In 2010, however, an increase occurred – individuals reporting that important political events escaped their attention and those who did not follow such events at all constituted 41% of the population. After 2010, interest in politics slightly decreased, only to rise in 2014 and in the first three-quarters of 2015, which may have been related to presidential and parliamentary elections. This increase in political interest was also observable in the form of the diminishing proportion of people slightly interested or uninterested in politics. This proportion decreased by 10% after 2013 to reach the level of 36% for the first three-quarters of 2015 (Kazanecki, 2015, pp. 1–2).

In a 2017 CBOS sociological survey, conducted on a representative random sample of 948 adult residents of Poland, an upward trend was observed for both "high" and "moderate" interest in politics. According to self-report data, 17% of respondents followed the events on the political scene with great interest at that time. The vast majority of Poles were moderately interested in politics or not interested in it at all. In the autumn of 2017, nearly every second respondent (45%) reported that they were moderately interested in politics, and two in five reported that politics was not particularly interesting to them (38%) (Cybulska, 2017, pp. 1–2).

In a CBOS survey published in 2020, in which Poles were asked to indicate their place in the social structure, a substantial majority of respondents rated their interest in politics as moderate (middle class – 50%, lower class – 43%, upper class – 38%). A slight interest or no interest whatsoever was reported by 43% of the Poles regarding themselves as members of the lower class, 31% of respondents from the middle class, and 26% of those from the upper class. Accordingly, a strong interest in politics was found most often among respondents regarding themselves as members of the upper class (36%), in every fifth respondent from the middle class (19%), and the least often in individuals from the lower class (13%) (Omyła-Rudzka, 2020, p. 6)

In the context of our research, which we will discuss below, what seems interesting is the findings presented by Marta Jas-Koziarkiewicz. Using qualitative methods to examine the contents of articles in Polish-language press, she analysed the Brexit-related narratives that appeared in Polish opinion weeklies in 2015 and 2016. Thus, she confirmed the link between the evaluation of that event in the weeklies and their political affiliations. This link was demonstrated for attitudes towards Brexit-related content, which was generally positive in Polish papers with right-wing leanings and negative in papers supporting the centre and the left of the political scene. No significant differences were found, however, as regards the causes and effects of Brexit identified by different editorial teams. Regardless of political affiliation, journalistic texts pointed to the same principal causes and main consequences of Britain's withdrawal from the European Union. The following were mentioned as the main causes of Brexit:

- David Cameron's political declaration made at the outset of the debate on the sense and purpose of the United Kingdom remaining in the European Union;
- mental differences between the inhabitants of the British Isles and continental Europe;
- opposition to the influx of migrants, especially those from the new EU member states (including Poland);
- the characteristic features of the European Union (bureaucracy, the enforcement of common principles);
- British people's strong attachment to sovereignty.

The common catalogue of expected consequences included a change in the balance of power in the international arena (with the strengthening of Russia's position), a change in Poland's situation in Europe, and the possible consequences for the European Union itself (Jas-Koziarkiewicz, 2019, pp. 84–92).

## The Communication of Brexit-Related Information Through the Media by Polish and British Authorities

Next, we will address the issue of Brexit-related information communicated by Polish and British authorities. In the autumn of 2019, we asked our respondents about their opinions concerning this problem. The sociological analysis also included respondents' views about the possible gains or losses resulting from the United Kingdom's withdrawal from the European Union. In our study we broke this problem down into several categories: consequences for the United Kingdom, Poland, the European Union, the respondent, and the respondent's family.

In our empirical research conducted in Oxford, London, and Swindon, we asked the following question: "What is your evaluation of the communication of current Brexit-related information by Polish and British authorities?" Nearly half of the respondents were critical about the actions of Polish authorities (poor – 35%, very poor – 14%), and every third respondent evaluated them positively (good – 26%, very good – 3.4%). One person in five had no clear opinion on the matter (21.6%) (Table 2.1).

The communication of current Brexit-related information by Polish authorities was evaluated more critically by respondents planning to leave the United Kingdom than by those planning to stay there permanently. Proportions were similar in the case of positive evaluations. Those who intended to remain permanently in the United Kingdom were the group with the highest percentage of individuals who felt unable to clearly evaluate Brexit-related media

*Table 2.1* Respondents' evaluation of the communication of Brexit-related information by Polish authorities and their self-reported intention to return to Poland

| Categories of answers | Within a few years | | In an indefinite future | | Never | | Hard to say | |
|---|---|---|---|---|---|---|---|---|
| | N | % | N | % | N | % | N | % |
| Very good | 5 | 3.5 | 6 | 3.2 | 4 | 4.6 | 6 | 3 |
| Good | 41 | 28.5 | 51 | 27.4 | 19 | 21.8 | 50 | 24.6 |
| Poor | 57 | 39.6 | 71 | 38.2 | 19 | 21.8 | 70 | 34.5 |
| Very poor | 17 | 11.8 | 30 | 16.1 | 15 | 17.2 | 25 | 12.3 |
| Hard to say | 24 | 16.7 | 28 | 15.1 | 30 | 34.5 | 52 | 25.6 |
| No answer | 0 | 0 | 0 | 0 | 0 | 0 | 0 | 0 |
| Total | 144 | 100 | 186 | 100 | 87 | 100 | 203 | 100 |

$\chi^2 = 2396$, $df = 12$, $p = 027$, $C = 0.190$

contents. Positive evaluations of how Polish authorities communicated information about Brexit were found predominantly among respondents planning to leave: women (M = 25.7%, W = 31.4%), white-collar workers (25.9%), respondents with 10–20 years of residence abroad behind them (30.8%), and migrants who had come to Britain between 2010 and 2019 (<10 years – 27%). With age, the positive evaluation of the quality of Polish authorities' Brexit-related information policy increased (<30 years – 19.1%, 30–39 years – 27.3%, 40–49 years – 31.4%, ≥50 years – 43.9%). Evaluations pertaining to this issue were more often negative among respondents planning to remain in the British Isles: men (M = 56.9%, W = 44.6%) and blue-collar workers (38.9%). The negative evaluation of Polish authorities' communication in this area decreased with the length of time spent abroad (<10 years – 57%, 10–20 years – 45.9%, >20 years – 38.1%) and with age (<30 years – 55.9%, 30–39 years – 52.3%, 40–49 years – 44.5%, ≥50 years – 40.9%).

The proportion of respondents with no opinion on this issue may inspire in-depth sociological research on Polish people's interest in politics in general. The subject of Brexit most certainly is among the crucial ones that the entire diaspora of migrants in Britain should be keenly interested in, as it is political and legal decisions that the fate of the people living there depends on. Putting aside the question of positive or negative evaluation of the Polish media coverage, it would be hard to defend the thesis that English-language or Polish-language media coverage of Brexit was not intensive enough. With a large measure of caution, it can therefore be concluded that Polish migrants' interest in current political issues is comparable to this kind of interest among their compatriots in Poland. What seems even more puzzling is the fact that the proportion of respondents with no opinion on Brexit was the highest among the migrants planning to stay in the British Isles. This may stem from a lack of interest in public affairs, from difficulties in defining the issues of direct interest to particular individuals, from the belief in a kind of social fatalism ("whatever is meant to be will be"), or from individuals' focus on the micro-social plane.

To sum up, it can be assumed that the protracted negotiations on the terms of Britain's withdrawal from the European Union and the repeated postponement of the date of this event caused an increase in anxiety and a kind of dismay among Polish people (Trąbka & Wermińska-Wiśnicka, 2020, p. 52). Moreover, if the level of confidence regarding a solution proposed by public authorities is low, and if the degree of competence in public affairs is minimal in a given society, then, quite naturally, interest in a given subject matter will be low or none at all (Czakon, 2015, p. 320).

In our research conducted in the autumn of 2019, we also asked respondents to evaluate the communication of Brexit-related information by British authorities. A characteristic pattern in the English-language news media was the gradual amplification and dissemination of selected issues linked with the United Kingdom's departure from the European Union, which included publicizing the widely debated topic of anti-immigration policy. This fact made the social transfer of knowledge rather subjective, selective, and therefore incomplete (Lavery, 2019, pp. 20–21). This provokes the question about the form in which English-language media coverage thus constructed became a direct source of knowledge and, consequently, opinions about Brexit.

A report by the Centre for Research in Communication and Culture at Loughborough University, devoted to the content analysis of English-language Brexit-related news in 2016, revealed that media coverage was restricted to the course of the referendum campaign and that the most significant substantive issues were economic interests and immigration control in Britain. Other issues, such as workers' rights, were almost entirely overlooked or even ignored in public debate in 2016; so was agriculture, even though the fate of this sector is strictly linked with the development of European Union's policy (Deacon, Harmer, Downey, Stanyer, & Wring, 2016a, p. 2).

The dominant subject in the news media in May 2016 was the course and procedure of the future referendum (29.1%). Other frequent topics were: the future shape of post-Brexit business and economy as well as trade between the United Kingdom and the European Union (20.1%); migration and border control (12.7%); constitutional, legal, and judicial issues (6.9%); public opinion research, including citizens' engagement in the referendum campaign (6.7%); territorial defence, the armed forces, and security (5.4%); employment (3.8%); corruption in the European Union (2.5%); health care (2,2%); the history and current activity of the European Union (1.7%); and the remaining issues (8.9%) (Deacon, Harmer, Downey, Stanyer, & Wring, 2016b).

In their further remarks, the authors of the report clearly stress the fact that media coverage at that time was marked by a considerable degree of "solidarity" in providing incomplete information about Brexit, manifesting itself, among other things, in the marginalisation of issues crucial for citizens, such as the consequences of leaving the European Union for agricultural policy, social security, or public services (Deacon, Harmer, Downey, Stanyer, & Wring, 2017a, 2017b).

An interesting analysis of recipients' trust in the media coverage of Brexit was conducted at the University of Oxford in February 2019. Respondents were asked to rate their confidence in Brexit coverage on a 10-point scale. It turned out that, for nearly all analysed sources of information, the level of confidence was higher among respondents reporting a preference for remaining in the European Union (5.96%) than among Eurosceptics (5.70%) (Fletcher & Selva, 2019, p. 4).

This being so, further analysis concerning the assessment of media coverage should be informed by the awareness of the "polarisation" of that coverage (Fletcher & Selva, 2019, p. 5), in which accumulating large amounts of data not only "allows for the micro-targeting of political messages" but also leads to a situation in which "such messages compete to render campaign commitments meaningless" (Krishnamurthy, 2017). The ways of communicating information may contribute to message distortion by the mass media, which may be a significant actor in political communication to the point of being capable of "redefining reality" (Piechocki, 2018, p. 23).

As we move on to our research conducted in October 2019, it should be noted that every second respondent evaluated the British media coverage of Brexit positively (very good – 10.6%, good – 37.9%), while four in ten evaluated it negatively (poor – 31.1%, very poor – 11.3%). Every ninth respondent was unable to give a clear opinion on the issue (8.9%), and one person did not answer the question at all (0.2%) (Table 2.2).

Every second respondent reporting an intention to remain abroad evaluated Brexit-related communication from British authorities positively. The most critical judges of the coverage of Britain's withdrawal from the European Union proved to be those who reported an intention to return to Poland within a few years. Brexit-related communication from British authorities was most often positively evaluated by respondents planning to stay permanently in the United Kingdom (unlike in the case of communication from Polish authorities), respondents with higher or secondary education (52.6% and 50.7%, respectively), white-collar workers (51.1%), and every second migrant who had begun their second decade of expatriate life (50.1%). As regards negative evaluations, they were more frequent among respondents planning to leave Britain; they were also reported by a majority of respondents with primary or basic vocational education (52.1%). As in the case of positive evaluations, the rate of negative opinions about the communication of Brexit-related information by British authorities turned out to be higher in the group of white-collar workers than among blue-collar workers (44.5% versus 40.6%).[1]

*Table 2.2* Respondents' evaluation of the communication of Brexit-related information by British authorities and their self-reported intention to return to Poland

| Categories of answers | Within a few years | | In an indefinite future | | Never | | Hard to say | |
|---|---|---|---|---|---|---|---|---|
| | N | % | N | % | N | % | N | % |
| Very good | 17 | 11.8 | 17 | 9.1 | 10 | 11.5 | 22 | 10.8 |
| Good | 43 | 29.9 | 76 | 40.9 | 35 | 40.2 | 81 | 39.9 |
| Poor | 51 | 35.4 | 59 | 31.7 | 22 | 25.3 | 61 | 30 |
| Very poor | 21 | 14.6 | 18 | 9.7 | 9 | 10.3 | 22 | 10.8 |
| Hard to say | 12 | 8.3 | 15 | 8.1 | 11 | 12.6 | 17 | 8.4 |
| No answer | 0 | 0 | 1 | 0.5 | 0 | 0 | 0 | 0 |
| Total | 144 | 100 | 186 | 100 | 87 | 100 | 203 | 100 |

$\chi^2 = 9.311$, $df = 12$, $p = 0.676$

## The Evaluation of Britain's Preparation for Brexit

It is unlikely that during the referendum anyone engaged in a thorough analysis of what consequences Brexit would have for the rights acquired by more than four million citizens, including three million European Union citizens living in the United Kingdom and more than one million British residents in EU countries (Gower, 2016). As a result, the unclear prospects regarding the manner of Britain's withdrawal from the European Union provoked questions about the degree of preparation for this "divorce." British political scientist Ben Stanley believes that the shock caused by the European Union's hard-line policy on Brexit has shown that Brussels may pursue the interest of the European organisation as a whole at the cost of the departing country.

> This is not going to be the beginning of the end, but the end of the beginning. This will be the moment when big changes [...] will begin, starting with the electoral system. Brexit will be followed by a review of what could have been done better. There will probably also be reflection on what else, in the light of the last three years, can be changed or improved in the country. We can see that the division in society and within political parties is deep.
>
> (Cichocki & Ben, 2019, p. 16)

For these reasons, it seemed reasonable to ask the respondents about their evaluation of Britain's preparation for leaving the European Union. The vast majority answered that this process should be evaluated negatively (as very poor – 66%, or poor – 23.9%), and every 15th respondent had no clear opinion on the matter (hard to say – 6.6%). In contrast, 21 respondents evaluated Britain's preparations for leaving the European Union as very good (3.4%) and one respondent assessed them as good (0.2%) (Table 2.3).

An overwhelming majority of respondents reporting an intention to return to Poland in an indefinite future rated the United Kingdom's preparation for Brexit negatively (the sum of "poor" and "very poor" evaluations – 94.1%), and so did the vast majority of those who had decided to remain in Britain (89.7%). An equally critical group proved to be the respondents who were undecided on whether to remain or return (87.7%) and those who wished to return to Poland as soon as possible (87.5%).

The United Kingdom chose Brexit mainly for economic reasons (Gardocka & Jagiełło, 2021, p. 279). This seems to explain the low evaluation of its preparation for "divorcing" the European Union both among the Poles planning to stay in Britain and among those planning to return. Brexit emerges as a problem common to these two groups. The Poles planning to leave the United Kingdom decide to remigrate due to the uncertainty about their situation abroad after Brexit, and those who plan to remain in the United Kingdom share the same uncertainty. It should be remembered that British

*Table 2.3* Evaluation of the United Kingdom's preparation for leaving the European Union and self-reported intention to return to Poland

| Categories of answers | Within a few years | | In an indefinite future | | Never | | Hard to say | |
|---|---|---|---|---|---|---|---|---|
| | N | % | N | % | N | % | N | % |
| Very good | 0 | 0 | 0 | 0 | 0 | 0 | 1 | 0.5 |
| Good | 8 | 5.6 | 2 | 1.1 | 5 | 5.7 | 6 | 3 |
| Poor | 27 | 18.8 | 51 | 27.4 | 16 | 18.4 | 54 | 26.6 |
| Very poor | 99 | 68.8 | 124 | 66.7 | 62 | 71.3 | 124 | 61.1 |
| Hard to say | 10 | 6.9 | 9 | 4.8 | 4 | 4.6 | 18 | 8.9 |
| No answer | 0 | 0 | 0 | 0 | 0 | 0 | 0 | 0 |
| Total | 144 | 100 | 186 | 100 | 87 | 100 | 203 | 100 |

$\chi^2 = 17.112$, $df = 12$, $p = 0.145$

migration policy after Brexit will be geared towards restrictions and selectivity (Brunarska, Kaczmarczyk, & Piekut, 2020, p. 96).

The factors mentioned as negatively affecting the integration of EU member states include different geographical zones of geopolitical interest (including different alliances); the complex organisation of the European Union, manifesting itself, for instance, in the lack of a clear decision-making centre; cultural discrepancies; and the common foreign and security policy lacking a homogeneous form and character (Grosse, 2009, pp. 3–8).

An important aspect in the interpretation of migrants' plans and options regarding their stay in Britain is their evaluation of and predictions concerning the effects of Brexit on their individual situation. In a sociological survey conducted in 2018 for the Department of Statistics of the National Bank of Poland, a clear majority of respondents (59.3%) asserted that Britain's departure from the European Union would not have much influence on their current situation and would not require any additional actions on their part. This result corresponds with the answers of those respondents who reported having permanent residence status or met the formal requirements to apply for it. The respondents who expected difficulties in the future but still did not plan to leave the United Kingdom accounted for 17.7% of the sample at that time, whereas 13.3% of the respondents in 2018 expected restrictions and felt the need to take steps, at the same time applying for settled or pre-settled status. Every tenth migrant indicated that their situation in the British job market might become so complicated in the future that they were not planning to stay there after Brexit (Chmielewska, Panuciak, & Strzelecki, 2019, p. 44).

Because a large majority of Polish migrants in the United Kingdom did not see any risks for their position in Britain after Brexit or had a plan on how to eliminate them (by applying for settled or pre-settled status), in the same sociological study they were asked how long they were planning to stay in the British Isles, assuming the realistic Brexit scenario. Most of them (84.1%) reported that these plans would not change. Returning earlier than planned was the option every tenth migrant was thinking of at the time – 10.3% (5.2% reported an intention to stay only until Brexit, while 5.1% decided to leave after Brexit – earlier than they had planned to). The remaining respondents (5.6%) had decided to extend their stay in the United Kingdom and reported having taken administrative steps in order to remain there after Brexit (Chmielewska et al., 2019, p. 45).

## Brexit – A Gain or a Loss?

In our study, in the autumn of 2019, we asked the respondents if Britain's departure from the European Union would be beneficial or detrimental to the European Union itself. Two in three respondents were sceptical about the future effects of Brexit for the European Union (65.8%), every seventh respondent asserted that Brexit would have no serious consequences for the European Union (13.7%), and 1.9% of respondents expected a beneficial effect of Brexit for Europe (1.9%). Every seventh respondent (13.9%) chose the "hard to say" answer, and every 20th (4.7%) did not answer this question at all (Table 2.4).

Those who remained in the United Kingdom expressed the opinion that Brexit would be of little consequence for the European Union more often than those who were planning to remigrate. More white-collar workers than blue-collar ones (71.2% versus 60.4%) saw Brexit as detrimental for the European Union; the percentage of respondents asserting that Brexit would be of little consequence for the European Union was the same in both groups (14.2%).

In our study, we asked the respondents if Britain's departure from the European Union would be beneficial or detrimental to Poland. Compared to the analogous question about the effect of Brexit on the European Union, the proportion of sceptics expecting negative consequences of Brexit for Poland was lower by eight percentage points (57.7% as against 65.8%), while the proportion of those who believed that Brexit would be of little significance for Poland was four percent higher (17.4%, as against 13.7%). The proportion of Brexit enthusiasts, claiming that Poland would benefit from the United Kingdom's withdrawal from the European Union was slightly higher as well (2.3%, as against 1.9% predicting benefits for the European Union). Compared to the previous question, there were also higher percentages of "hard to say" answers (13.9% versus 16.1%) and missing answers (6.5%) (Table 2.5).

Respondents turned out to be slightly less sceptical about the consequences of Brexit for Poland than they were about its effects for the European Union as a whole. A fear that the United Kingdom's departure from the European Union would have negative consequences for Poland was expressed by three in five respondents planning to return to Poland in an indefinite future and those undecided about whether to return to Poland or remain in the United

*Table 2.4* Evaluation of the consequences of the United Kingdom's departure from the European Union for the European Union and self-reported intention to return to Poland

| Categories of answers | Within a few years | | In an indefinite future | | Never | | Hard to say | |
|---|---|---|---|---|---|---|---|---|
| | N | % | N | % | N | % | N | % |
| Beneficial | 4 | 2.8 | 5 | 2.7 | 1 | 1.1 | 2 | 1 |
| Of little consequence | 21 | 14.6 | 23 | 12.4 | 18 | 20.7 | 23 | 11.3 |
| Detrimental | 87 | 60.4 | 123 | 66.1 | 56 | 64.4 | 142 | 70 |
| Hard to say | 21 | 14.6 | 25 | 13.4 | 11 | 12.6 | 29 | 14.3 |
| No answer | 11 | 7.6 | 10 | 5.4 | 1 | 1.1 | 7 | 3.4 |
| Total | 144 | 100 | 186 | 100 | 87 | 100 | 203 | 100 |

$\chi^2 = 7.551$, $df = 9$, $p = 0.580$

*Table 2.5* Evaluation of the consequences of the United Kingdom's departure from the European Union for Poland and self-reported intention to return to Poland

| Categories of answers | Within a few years | | In an indefinite future | | Never | | Hard to say | |
|---|---|---|---|---|---|---|---|---|
| | N | % | N | % | N | % | N | % |
| Beneficial | 6 | 4.2 | 5 | 2.7 | 2 | 2.3 | 1 | 0.5 |
| Of little consequence | 29 | 20.1 | 34 | 18.3 | 16 | 18.4 | 29 | 14.3 |
| Detrimental | 79 | 54.9 | 109 | 58.6 | 51 | 58.6 | 119 | 58.6 |
| Hard to say | 19 | 13.2 | 25 | 13.4 | 14 | 16.1 | 42 | 20.7 |
| No answer | 11 | 7.6 | 13 | 7 | 4 | 4.6 | 12 | 5.9 |
| Total | 144 | 100 | 186 | 100 | 87 | 100 | 203 | 100 |

$\chi^2 = 7.551$, $df = 9$, $p = 0.580$

Kingdom permanently (58.6% in both cases), as well as by slightly fewer respondents reporting an intention to return to Poland in the nearest future (54.9%). However, negative consequences of Brexit for Poland were more often stressed by migrants planning to remain in Britain permanently.

No benefits for Poland as a result of Brexit (the "of little consequence" response) were predicted more often by the respondents who intended to stay in the United Kingdom or postponed their departure, by nearly two-thirds of white-collar workers (65.3%), and by every second white-collar worker (51%). Considerably more blue-collar workers than white-collar workers (19.4% versus 12%) had no opinion on what effect Brexit, in preparation at that time, would have on Poland.

The next stage of our study into the attitudes of Poles towards Brexit concerned the evaluation of Britain's withdrawal from the European Union from the perspective of the United Kingdom itself. Three in four respondents believed that Brexit was detrimental (73.2%), while every tenth migrant held the opposite view (9.5%). A low proportion of respondents (3.1%) maintained that Brexit would have no influence on the United Kingdom, every tenth respondent (10%) admitted that they had no clear opinion on the matter, and 4.2% of Polish migrants gave no answer (Table 2.6).

The most sceptical group regarding the perceived value of Brexit for the United Kingdom proved to be the respondents who intended to return to Poland in an indefinite future (78.5%); scepticism was slightly less frequent among those who were planning to remain abroad permanently (72.4%) and among the undecided ones (71.9%). Scepticism, which consisted in expecting negative effects, was shared by two in three respondents reporting an intention to return to Poland in the nearest future (68.8%).

Negative consequences of Brexit for Britain were more often indicated by individuals determined to remain there than by those planning to remigrate, by women more often than by men (M = 66.1%, W = 77.8%), by eight out of ten white-collar workers (79.6%) and seven out of ten blue-collar workers (70.1%). Those who saw Brexit as a chance for Britain were respondents planning to return to Poland, more often men than women (M = 14.7%, W = 7%), every tenth blue-collar worker (9.7%), and every 11th white-collar worker (8.8%).

In the last question concerning the group of issues analysed here, we asked the respondents if Britain's departure from the European Union was beneficial or detrimental to them and their families. Nearly every second respondent (49.2%) expressed a fear that, for them and their family, British people's decision to leave the European Union would have negative consequences, and 22.6% of the respondents indicated that Brexit was of no consequence to them and their loved ones. Slightly fewer respondents reported that they had no clear opinion on the matter (21.9%), and only five respondents saw Brexit as a chance for themselves and their families (0.8%). Almost every 20th respondent gave no answer to this question (5.5%) (Table 2.7).

Table 2.6 Evaluation of the consequences of the United Kingdom's departure from the European Union for the United Kingdom and self-reported intention to return to Poland

| Categories of answers | Within a few years | | In an indefinite future | | Never | | Hard to say | |
|---|---|---|---|---|---|---|---|---|
| | N | % | N | % | N | % | N | % |
| Beneficial | 16 | 11.1 | 16 | 8.6 | 8 | 9.2 | 19 | 9.4 |
| Of little consequence | 7 | 4.9 | 2 | 1.1 | 3 | 3.4 | 7 | 3.4 |
| Detrimental | 99 | 68.8 | 146 | 78.5 | 63 | 72.4 | 146 | 71.9 |
| Hard to say | 13 | 9 | 18 | 9.7 | 10 | 11.5 | 21 | 10.3 |
| No answer | 9 | 6.3 | 4 | 2.2 | 3 | 3.4 | 10 | 4.9 |
| Total | 144 | 100 | 186 | 100 | 87 | 100 | 203 | 100 |

$\chi^2 = 5.972$, $df = 9$, $p = 0.743$

*Table 2.7* Evaluation of the consequences of the United Kingdom's departure from the European Union for oneself and one's family and self-reported intention to return to Poland

| Categories of answers | Within a few years | | In an indefinite future | | Never | | Hard to say | |
|---|---|---|---|---|---|---|---|---|
| | N | % | N | % | N | % | N | % |
| Beneficial | 1 | 0.7 | 1 | 0.5 | 2 | 2.3 | 1 | 0.5 |
| Of little consequence | 34 | 23.6 | 36 | 19.4 | 22 | 25.3 | 48 | 23.6 |
| Detrimental | 64 | 44.4 | 104 | 55.9 | 38 | 43.7 | 99 | 48.8 |
| Hard to say | 33 | 22.9 | 38 | 20.4 | 22 | 25.3 | 43 | 21.2 |
| No answer | 12 | 8.3 | 7 | 3.8 | 3 | 3.4 | 12 | 5.9 |
| Total | 144 | 100 | 186 | 100 | 87 | 100 | 203 | 100 |

$\chi^2 = 7.487$, $df = 9$, $p = 0.587$

Fears that Brexit would have negative consequences for the respondents and their families were more often reported by women (M = 42.7%, W = 53.9%) and by individuals aged over 40 (40–49 years – 55%, ≥50 years – 54.5%). Likewise, respondents with higher education more often viewed their future after Brexit pessimistically (master's degree – 56%, bachelor's degree – 55.9%). Considerably more white-collar workers than blue-collar ones expressed fears regarding Brexit (56.6% versus 45.8%).

Every fourth man and every fifth woman reported a belief that Brexit would be of little consequence for them and their families (M = 25.7%, W = 20.6%); this view was held most often by the youngest participants in the sociological survey (<30 years – 38.2%) and by respondents with primary or basic vocational education (29.2%). The belief that Brexit would be of little consequence to them was reported by every fifth blue-collar worker (20.8%) and by a slightly higher proportion of white-collar workers (23.4%).

## Summary

The aim of this part of the study was to determine Polish migrants' views on the communication of Brexit-related information by Polish and British authorities and to explore their evaluation of Britain's preparation for leaving the European Union. Some of the research presented here was also devoted to our respondents' opinions concerning the consequences of Brexit for the European Union, Poland, the United Kingdom, and the respondents themselves as well as their families. The empirical analysis performed allows for making a summary and formulating several key conclusions.

It is worth noting that every second respondent critically evaluated the Polish coverage of Brexit and that this was more often done by respondents planning to remain in the United Kingdom than by those planning to leave that country. Respondents evaluated the British coverage somewhat higher than the Polish coverage of Brexit-related issues, with British media coverage being rated higher by the Poles determined to remain in the United Kingdom after Brexit and more sceptically by those planning to return to return to their country of origin. A vast majority of respondents were critical about the United Kingdom's preparation for Brexit. In this case, low ratings were given both by respondents planning to remain in the British Isles and by those planning to return.

In the questions about the consequences of Brexit, two-thirds of the respondents answered that this political decision was detrimental to the European Union. Respondents who intended to remain in the country of settlement more often claimed that Brexit would not have a significant effect on the European Union. When answering the question about post-Brexit consequences for Poland, respondents slightly less strongly pointed to the possible negative consequences stemming from the London–Brussels divorce. Negative consequences for Poland were more often predicted by migrants planning to remain in the United Kingdom, while those planning to return more often expressed neutral opinions, asserting that Brexit would be of little significance for Poland.

When answering the question about the consequences of Brexit for the United Kingdom, a substantial majority of respondents expressed a belief that leaving the European Union would have a detrimental effect, but it should be stressed that, in response to this question, every tenth respondent asserted that Brexit would benefit Britain in certain ways. This is worth noting because, with such a high level of scepticism about British people's decision made in 2016, in the case of no other question about the consequences of the United Kingdom's departure from the European Union were the possible benefits emphasised so strongly. In other words, a high percentage of respondents saw Brexit as having positive consequences for the United Kingdom.

In the last question in this series, we asked about post-Brexit consequences for the respondents themselves and their families. Every second respondent reported that they feared the negative consequences of the 2016 referendum, and the percent of those who claimed that Brexit would affect neither them nor their families was two times lower than in an analogous question included in the report of the National Bank of Poland.

Looking at the issues analysed from an even more general perspective, one can say that the Poles planning to remain in the United Kingdom after Brexit approached British people's decision to leave the European Union more leniently than those planning to return to Poland, although they were also critical of Britain's preparation for Brexit and the related news coverage as well as pessimistic about the consequences that they subjectively expected the United Kingdom's departure from the European Union to have for them.

So, the question arises: how big a push factor was the prospect of Brexit to return to Poland? An attempt to answer can be found in analysing migrants' reactions to the previous global financial crisis in 2007–2009. Contrary to analysts' expectations, many Polish migrants stayed abroad (Jancewicz, Kloc-Nowak, & Pszczółkowska, 2020). At that time, sociological research on the Polish migrant diaspora showed decreased short-term mobility and the advantage of long-term migrants among Poles in the main EU countries (Janicka & Kaczmarczyk, 2016). In addition, it has been shown that the length of stay, higher earnings, and the fact of owning properties abroad correlate with decisions to stay in the country of settlement of Poles, regardless of global economic crises (Jancewicz & Markowski, 2021). This confirms the thesis that migrants more anchored in the place of their life are not willing to re-emigrate despite socio-economic concerns (Jancewicz et al., 2020). In the context of Brexit, it should be expected that migrants who have invested in their professional competencies in the United Kingdom and have achieved employment stability will not decide to leave hastily. Their decision to stay in the United Kingdom may be more beneficial in the long term than returning to their country of origin.

# Note

1 Blue-collar workers avoided providing a clear evaluation three times more often than white-collar workers, choosing the "hard to say" answer (12.2% versus 4.4%), hence the similar percentages for positive and negative evaluations.

# References

Babik, Wiesław. (2012). Kultura informacyjna. Spojrzenie z punktu widzenia ekologii informacji. *Bibliotheca Nostra. Śląski Kwartalnik Naukowy*, 2 (2), 31–40. https://ruj.uj.edu.pl/xmlui/bitstream/handle/item/25172/babik_kultura_informacyjna_spojrzenie_z_punktu_widzenia_ekologii_informacji_2012.pdf?sequence=1&isAllowed=y (2022-03-26)

Brunarska, Zuzanna, Kaczmarczyk, Paweł, & Piekut, Aneta. (2020). Postawy wobec imigrantów w «starych» i «nowych» krajach imigracyjnych. Czy historia imigracji ma znaczenie? In Sztabiński, P. B., Przybysz, D., & Sztabiński, F. (Eds.), *Polska – Europa. Wyniki Europejskiego Sondażu Społecznego 2002–2018/19*, 92–112. Warszawa: Wydawnictwo IFiS PAN. https://ifispan.pl/wp-content/uploads/2021/06/Polska-Europa.-Wyniki-Europejskiego-Sondazu-Spolecznego-2002-2018_19.pdf (2023-02-06)

Chmielewska, Iza, Panuciak, Adam, & Strzelecki, Paweł. (2019). *Polacy pracujący za granicą w 2018 r. Raport z badania* (Polski, N. B. Ed.). Warszawa: Departament Statystyki NBP. https://www.nbp.pl/publikacje/migracyjne/polacy_pracujacy_za_granica_2018.pdf (2023-01-12)

Cichocki, Marek A., & Ben, Stanley. (2019). Brexit i rewolucja populizmu w Europie. *Sprawy Międzynarodowe*, 72 (2), 9–16. https://doi.org/10.35757/SM.2019.72.21 (2023-03-24)

Cybulska, Agnieszka. (2017). *Monolog, dialog czy kłótnia – Polaków rozmowy o polityce Komunikat z badań CBOS*, 153/2017, 1–18. Warszawa: Centrum Badania Opinii Społecznej. https://www.cbos.pl/SPISKOM.POL/2017/K_153_17.PDF (2022-03-22)

Czakon, Piotr. (2015). Zaangażowani i obojętni wobec działalności publicznej. Teoria kultury politycznej jako narzędzie analizy postaw wobec sfery publicznej. *Pisma Humanistyczne*, 13, 313–327. https://www.ceeol.com/search/viewpdf?id=422041 (2023-02-06)

Deacon, David, Harmer, Emily, Downey, John, Stanyer, James, & Wring, Dominic. (2016a). *UK news coverage of the 2016 EU referendum: Report 1 (6–18 May 2016)*, 1–16. Loughborough: Loughborough University. https://repository.lboro.ac.uk/articles/report/UK_news_coverage_of_the_2016_EU_Referendum_Report_3_6_May_8_June_2016_/9471278 (2023-02-06)

Deacon, David, Harmer, Emily, Downey, John, Stanyer, James, & Wring, Dominic. (2016b). *UK news coverage of the 2016 EU Referendum: Report 2 (19 May–June 2016)*, 1–15. Loughborough: Loughborough University. https://blog.lboro.ac.uk/wp-content/uploads/sites/23/2016/06/eu-referendum-media-analysis-report-2.pdf (2023-02-06)

Deacon, David, Harmer, Emily, Downey, John, Stanyer, James, & Wring, Dominic. (2017a). *UK news coverage of the 2016 EU Referendum: Report 3 (6 May–8 June 2016)*, 1–16. Loughborough: Loughborough University. https://repository.lboro.ac

.uk/articles/report/UK_news_coverage_of_the_2016_EU_Referendum_Report_3
_6_May_8_June_2016_/9471278 (2023-02-06)

Deacon, David, Harmer, Emily, Downey, John, Stanyer, James, & Wring, Dominic. (2017b). *UK news coverage of the 2016 EU Referendum: Report 4 (6 May–15 June 2016)*, 1–10. Loughborough: Loughborough University. https://repository.lboro.ac.uk/articles/report/UK_news_coverage_of_the_2016_EU_Referendum_Report_4 _6_May_15_June_2016_/9470801 (2023-02-06)

Dejneka, Piotr. (2019). *Populizm a sfera publiczna: czy populizm zrewitalizuje sferę publiczną w Europie?* Warszawa: Wydawnictwo Naukowe UKSW.

Eurobarometr. (2018). *Opinia publiczna w Unii Europejskiej Standardowy Eurobarometr 90*, 1–12. Warszawa: Komisja Europejska. https://docplayer.pl /132519401-Standardowy-eurobarometr-90-opinia-publiczna-w-unii-europejskiej .html (2023-02-06)

Fedorowicz, M., & Skipietrow, Natalia. (2017). *W jakim stopniu wiedza jest czynnikiem współkształtującym dyskurs o Europie*, 1–20. https://www.batory.org.pl/upload/ files/Programy%20operacyjne/Otwarta%20Europa/Czesc%202%20-%20Wiedza .pdf (2022-03-21)

Fletcher, R., & Selva, M. (2019). *How Brexit Referendum voters use news*, 1–8. Oxford: Reuters Institute for the Study of Journalism. https://eclass.uoa.gr/modules /document/file.php/MEDIA326/How%20Brexit%20Referendum%20Voters %20Use%20News_Richard%20Fletcher%20and%20Meera%20Selva.pdf (2023-01-06)

Gardocka, Teresa, & Jagiełło, Dariusz. (2021). Unia Europejska – Wspólny los Polski i Litwy, czy indywidualne wyzwanie? *Krytyka prawa. Niezależne studia nad prawem*, 13 (1), 271–280. https://www.ceeol.com/search/viewpdf?id=1011587 (2023-02-06)

Gower, Melanie. (2016). *Leaving the EU: How might people currently exercising free movement rights be affected*. http://researchbriefings.parliament.uk/ ResearchBriefing/Summary/CBP-7525 (2021-11-20)

Grosse, Tomasz Grzegorz. (2009). O słabości polityki zagranicznej Unii Europejskiej. *Analizy Natolińskie*, 40 (8), 1–19. https://www.natolin.edu.pl/wp-content/themes/ cen/includes/download.php?f=15692 (2022-02-01)

Habermas, Jürgen. (1989). *The structural transformation of the public sphere*. Cambridge,: The MIT Press.

Hułas, Maciej. (2019). *Decydować samemu: sfera publiczna jako locus autonomii według Jürgena Habermasa*. Lublin: Wydawnictwo KUL.

Jancewicz, Barbara, Kloc-Nowak, Weronika, & Pszczółkowska, Dominika. (2020). Push, pull and Brexit: Polish migrants' perceptions of factors discouraging them from staying in the UK. *Central and Eastern European Migration Review*, 9 (1). https://www.ceeol.com/search/article-detail?id=881264

Jancewicz, Barbara, & Markowski, Stefan. (2021). Economic turbulence and labour migrants' mobility intentions: Polish migrants in the United Kingdom, Ireland, the Netherlands and Germany 2009–2016. *Journal of Ethnic and Migration Studies*, 47 (17), 3928–3947. http://doi.org/10.1080/1369183X.2019.1656059

Janicka, Anna, & Kaczmarczyk, Paweł. (2016). Mobilities in the crisis and post-crisis times: Migration strategies of Poles on the EU labour market. *Journal of Ethnic and Migration Studies*, 42 (10), 1693–1710. http://doi.org/10.1080/1369183X.2016 .1162350

Jas-Koziarkiewicz, Marta. (2019). Polish Opinion Weeklies about Brexit in 2015 and 2016. *Online Journal Modelling the New Europe* (29), 78–107. http://dx.doi.org/10 .24193/ojmne.2019.294 (2022-03-25)

Kazanecki, Wojciech. (2015). *Zainteresowanie polityką i poglądy polityczne w latach 1989–2015. Deklaracje ludzi młodych na tle ogółu badanych Komunikat z badań CBOS*, 16/2021, 1–9. Warszawa: Centrum Badania Opinii Społecznej (2023-02-06)

Krishnamurthy, Vidya. (2017). *Q&A with Kelly Born: Getting beyond disinformation*. https://hewlett.org/qa-kelly-born-getting-beyond-disinformation/ (2020-01-10)

Lavery, Sioned Ellen. (2019). *A very English Brexit: A comparative analysis of the immigration debate in the news media of the four UK nations*. Sydney: University of Sydney. https://ses.library.usyd.edu.au/bitstream/handle/2123/19798/Lavery _Final_Thesis.pdf?sequence=1&isAllowed=y. https://ses.library.usyd.edu.au/ bitstream/handle/2123/19798/Lavery_Final_Thesis.pdf?sequence=1&isAllowed=y (2023-01-06)

Marchand, Donald A., Kettinger, William J., & Rollins, John D. (2002). *Information orientation: The link to business performance*. Oxford: Oxford University Press. https://doi.org/10.1093/acprof:oso/9780199252213 01001 (2023-03-25)

Misztal, Wojciech. (2015). Dialog obywatelski. In Mariański, J. (Ed.), *Leksykon socjologii moralności. Podstawy – Teorie – Badania – Perspektywy*, 117–124. Kraków: Nomos.

Ochman, Andrzej. (2015). Medialna sfera publiczna według Jürgena Habermasa. *Studia Paradyskie*, 25, 147–168. https://bibliotekanauki.pl/articles/516497.pdf (2023-02-06)

Omyła-Rudzka, Małgorzata. (2020). *Klasa niższa, średnia i wyższa. Charakterystyka w oparciu o autoidentyfikacje Polaków Komunikat z badań CBOS*, 61/2020, 1–12. Warszawa: Centrum Badania Opinii Społecznej. https://www.cbos.pl/SPISKOM .POL/2020/K_061_20.PDF (2023-02-06)

Piechocki, Marcin. (2018). *Świat Przedstawiony. Sposoby kreowania rzeczywistości społeczno-politycznej w portalu fronda.pl*. Poznań: Wydawnictwo Naukowe Uniwersytetu Adama Mickiewicza.

Szymańska, Agnieszka. (2016). *Europa dziennikarzy: dyplomacja mediów i (post) narodowa Europa w świetle wypowiedzi niemieckich dziennikarzy prasowych*. Kraków: Wydawnictwo Uniwersytetu Jagiellońskiego. https://www.researchgate .net/publication/333115956_Europa_dziennikarzy_Dyplomacja_mediow_i _postnarodowa_Europa_w_swietle_wypowiedzi_niemieckich_dziennikarzy _prasowych (2023-01-06)

Tarde, Gabriel. (1904). *Opinia i tłum*. Warszawa: Nakład Gebethnera i Wolfa.

Trąbka, Agnieszka, & Wermińska-Wiśnicka, Iga. (2020). Niejednoznaczny wpływ Brexitu na życie młodych Polaków w Wielkiej Brytanii. *Studia Migracyjne – Przegląd Polonijny*, 178 (4), 49–70. http://dx.doi.org/10.4467/25444972SMPP .2038.12775 (2023-05-01)

# III Polish People's Motives for Staying in the United Kingdom after Brexit

## Introduction

Migratory mobility is an interesting area for observation and analysis. This is because, on the one hand, it is treated as the realisation of the basic human right to choose the place of residence and work, while on the other hand the migration reality generates many problems and barriers – juridical, social, and cultural – which migrants have to face. What undoubtedly generates new challenges is the unprecedented phenomenon of the European Union being left by a member state that, for many years, used to be among the top absorbers of migration, especially economic migration. The contemporary "migration of peoples" is analysed primarily in the context of increasing globalisation. The characteristics of the global community currently in the making include unlimited freedom of movement from one society to another, freedom of temporarily staying in the place of settlement, and possibilities of returning without significant loss for the individual. In this context, it seems interesting to analyse an important aspect of Polish people making plans regarding their further residence in the United Kingdom and the possibilities of staying there with the limitation of post-Brexit migration opportunities in prospect.

## Possible Migration Scenarios

Based on quantitative research conducted in 2015 in the United Kingdom, Wioletta Szymczak distinguished the following migration scenarios:

- bilaterally open (no precise plans regarding emigration or return);
- unilaterally open (individuals who intended to return soon at the time of their arrival and had no specific plans connected with their emigration, or individuals who had specific goals when emigrating and at the same time kept their options open about remaining in the country of settlement in the future);
- bilaterally closed (a precisely defined goal of emigration and specific plans of leaving or remaining in the United Kingdom) (Szymczak, 2018, pp. 21–25).

DOI: 10.4324/9781003449843-3

On this basis, the Lublin-based sociologist distinguished factors that encouraged migrants to remain in the United Kingdom by creating better conditions and opportunities for achieving what a given individual perceived as well-being. In the Polish context, this could mean the possibility of achieving security and financial stability, understood both as an autotelic goal and as an instrumental one necessary for the fulfilment of other needs or aspirations in life (Szymczak, 2018, p. 35). In practice, the decision to stay in the country of settlement or to return to the country of origin may stem from various reasons on the *macro* (a market crisis, the improvement of the economic situation in Poland), *meso* (a change in the attitude of the local community towards Polish people, an opportunity to go to university in Britain), and *micro* levels (loss of job, a preference for having one's children educated in Poland, looking after one's family members) (Karolak, 2015, p. 42).

As regards return migration, Krystyna Iglicka proposed to distinguish:

- forced returns (loss of job, no possibility of finding a job, family problems); and
- occasional returns, being an interlude before emigrating again to the country one previously lived in or to a different country.

Iglicka refers to the latter type of returns as the *migration loop trap* (2010a). Return migrants' most frequent strategies in the population she analysed were re-emigration strategies that consisted in going back to the country one had just returned from due to "disappointment" with the reality encountered in the country of origin (Iglicka, 2010a, p. 86). In this context, it can be assumed that the fears associated with returning include a fear of "starting from scratch" in the case of deciding to return to the country of origin, disappointment with it, and the need to make another decision to emigrate.

In her study on Polish migrants in Britain, Kathy Burrell from the University of Liverpool mentions a reversal in the direction of the *brain waste* phenomenon – even though young and talented migrants could not make use of their qualifications in the country of origin, the characteristic mobility they showed in their lives released in them an energetic attitude to life and professional activity (Burrell, 2017). Thus, emigration opportunities and unhindered access to work abroad protect individuals against exclusion from the job market and offer them a real chance of improving their life situation (Ślebarska, 2009, p. 154).

## The Most Frequent Reasons for Returning to Poland and for Staying Abroad

The family policy in the United Kingdom is usually referred to as liberal. Appropriate instruments of social policy are an element of the welfare state. Britain provides considerably more social services and benefits than Poland does. In the United Kingdom, the eligibility criteria are considerably more flexible and egalitarian, since people at risk of social exclusion and with an income below the poverty line have the right to receive financial benefits before others (Pujer, 2017, pp. 24–25). This is an important factor that argues in favour of remaining in Britain permanently in the case of people in the economically non-productive age or oscillating near the threshold of social dysfunctions. Based on the overall Eurostat statistical data published in March 2020, concerning issues such as income and living conditions, analysts generated ratios of average gross individual retirement pension for the 65–74 age group to median gross salary for the 50–59 age group, with other social benefits excluded. The closer the ratio was to 1.00, the closer the average pension was to the median salary (2010: Poland – 0.57, the United Kingdom – 0.48; 2015: 0.62 versus 0.50; 2018: 0.60 versus 0.56). This ratio should be analysed with some caution because it does not take account of the differences in social benefits and earnings between the countries compared. It therefore fluctuates slightly in Poland, while in the United Kingdom it exhibits a mild upward trend. In a way, this can explain the reasons for remaining in the country of settlement after retiring due to the predictability of the situation of people in the post-productive age (Eurostat, 2020).

As a result, it is legitimate to ask about migrants' reasons for remaining in Britain and compare them with their reasons for deciding to emigrate from Poland. What also seems quite interesting is the juxtaposition of migrants' declarations with their administrative actions – namely, the specific steps they took to secure further legal residence in the British Isles after Brexit. On this basis, it is possible to draw conclusions regarding the types of migrants – they will be differentiated chiefly by their reasons for returning, postponing the decision, or remaining in the country of settlement.

In the second quarter of 2008, Statistics Poland (GUS) asked Poles about their reasons for emigrating. The survey included as many as 42,700 respondents. The institution's experts stress, however, that the report was prepared mainly for job market research purposes, which is why its results should be approached with caution as presenting a limited spectrum of reasons behind return migration. In the analysed survey, migrants indicated the following as the most important reasons for returning: the end of the period they had planned to spend abroad (20%), the end of a contract (19%), and missing their family (16%) (Iglicka, 2010b, p. 94).

The research conducted among Poles in the United Kingdom and Ireland in 2007 sheds some light on the issues discussed here. The factor discouraging migrants most strongly from returning to Poland is the work culture. Migrants, especially highly qualified ones and those reporting an intention to start their own business in the future, complained about the negative attitude ("parochialism") and the traditionalism of behaviour in the Polish job market and the discrimination of women there. Respondents also mentioned the general issue of how citizens were treated in Poland and how people treated one another: the lack of trust, the lack of friendly attitude, and the lack of interest in the other person (Garapich & Osipovič, 2007, p. 19).

Towards the end of 2013 and at the beginning of 2014, Mateusz Karolak conducted 22 autobiographical narrative interviews with migrants who had returned from Britain to Poland and with return migrants who were planning to emigrate again after at least half a year in Poland. Based on the results of his research, he identified two types of goals which caused migrants to return once achieved.

• instrumental goals (return as an investment; return as a test); and
• non-instrumental goals (return as a moral choice; return as a refuge).

The author challenges the economic theories interpreting return as a consequence of a rational individual decision based on the calculation of economic gains and losses; he insists that not in every case is it possible to speak of one reason for returning to the country of origin, much less about an exclusively economic reason (Karolak, 2015, pp. 43–49).

A 2014 report of the Migration Research Committee of the Polish Academy of Sciences (PAN) revealed that an important factor influencing the decision to remain in Britain was the compensation of employees, still attractive compared to that in Poland (Slany & Solga, 2014, p. 25). This corresponds with the hard data published by Eurostat. Analysing average workers' wages per year in the United Kingdom before deducting income tax and insurance contributions, one can observe a clear decrease in 2009 compared to 2008 and a slow increase again from 2010 (€36,386, €40,171, and €38,284, respectively) (Eurostat, 2020). The second factor identified in the PAN report as transforming temporary migration into permanent is the family unity argument:

> Research indicates that temporary migration increasingly often becomes a way of life for Polish families, in which periods of *being together* alternate with much longer periods of *being apart*. Despite temporary separation, physically absent migrants are usually present all the time in the life of their families remaining in the home country. Research also shows that families with at least one migrant more and more often decide to emigrate permanently. The economic migration of one of the spouses leads to the decision to unite the family and settle abroad.
>
> (Slany & Solga, 2014, p. 28)

Both older and younger people sooner or later refused to come to terms with the prospect of migration-related separation, hence their frequent choices to join their families (White, 2011, pp. 91–92). Exploring British reality, Małgorzata Irek goes a little further in her reflection and refers to Polish people's refusal to accept the Western model of the British family, with considerably looser ties and moral obligations, as a case of cultural misunderstanding;

in this light, their stronger nostalgia for the loved ones abroad and their desire to join their family members currently living in the country of settlement seem to be more understandable (Irek, 2011, p. 17).

Another argument analysed in the report is to remain in the country of settlement due to one of the typical features of the most recent migration – the ease of keeping one's job and at the same time the possibility of pursuing further professional development. Poles find it easier to acquire economic, cultural, and social capital outside their home country, not only through participation in formal education systems (studies, educational programmes) but also through work and participation in community life (Wódka, 2017). The report stresses that it is non-formal (training courses) and informal (training for a job in the workplace, multicultural contacts) ways of acquiring human capital when living abroad that are particularly important because they concern the vast majority of Polish migrants (Slany & Solga, 2014, pp. 62–63).

Let us also look at other studies. The results of quantitative research on the functioning of children and adolescents returning from emigration, published in 2015, revealed the difficulties and challenges faced by entire families returning to Poland. These include:

* the child's strong attachment to the place of settlement (*attachment theory*);
* children's emotional difficulties associated with the migration experience;
* school problems, including an inadequate command of the Polish language and curricular differences; and
* cultural differences (Grzymała-Moszczyńska, Grzymała-Moszczyńska, Drulik, & Szydłowska, 2015, pp. 38–53).

Publications also provide general observations made by numerous Polish migrants that argue in favour of remaining in the British Isles, which concern issues such as tolerance and open-mindedness in Britain (Rabikowska, 2010, pp. 289–296), ordinary interpersonal relations, or even everyday politeness rooted in the Anglo-Saxon tradition (Rabikowska & Burrell, 2009, pp. 214–230).

## Why Stay in the United Kingdom? The Results of Our Research

In our research project, with the aim of discussing the socioeconomic determinants of Polish migrants' attitudes to Britain's withdrawal from the European Union, we asked respondents what influenced their decisions to remain in the British Isles. The respondents usually indicated the prospect of higher earnings (47.3%). Many of them saw the option of remaining abroad as one that offered greater opportunities for personal development, including professional advancement (36.6%). Reluctance to return to the country of origin due to fears about having to organize many aspects of residence there anew ("starting a life in Poland almost *from scratch*") was indicated by 34.4% of respondents, and every third reported a willingness to stay in the country of settlement due to easier access to the job market (33.2%). Slightly fewer respondents indicated cultural openness and higher tolerance in Britain (25.8%). This is where a distinction between two types of migration becomes visible:

*   modernist migration (a quest for "new" values); and
*   conservative migration (protecting values) (Banaś, 2005, pp. 18–19).

Fears related to children's problems with adaptation at school in Poland in the case of returning were expressed by 17.6% of respondents, and every eighth migrant reported that what encouraged them to stay abroad was a better functioning social and health insurance system (12.7%). Other reasons also argued in favour of returning but were not included in the set of answers (11.8%), for example, six respondents mentioned "family" and "children's illness." The remaining answers in the "other" category also revolved around family (grandchildren; I was born in England; married to an English woman; children born here; children have started English education) or professional and economic issues (lack of work ethics in Poland; pension; mortgage to pay, studies, my own business, sedate life, a better future for the children) (Table 3.1).

The answer suggesting the prospect of higher earnings in Britain was indicated most often in the group of respondents who had already decided to return to Poland and least often in the group of migrants planning to settle permanently in the United Kingdom. It can be assumed that there was a change of motivation for emigrating to and remaining in Britain among the migrants reporting an intention to settle there permanently, since one of the key reasons for emigrating years before had been economic considerations, whereas in the case of reasons for staying abroad this argument was not indicated by respondents as a primary one. The respondents who intended to remain in the United Kingdom most often indicated the argument of greater opportunities for personal and professional development (55.2%). Fears about starting a life in Poland almost from scratch in the case of choosing the return scenario were usually experienced by respondents reporting an intention to return in an indefinite future. What may be surprising is that the respondents who had already decided to stay permanently in Britain would be the least afraid to return.

In the case of individuals who decided to settle in the United Kingdom, the arguments in favour of remaining in the country of settlement were:

*   greater social tolerance;
*   easier access to the job market; and
*   better access to retirement benefits, welfare benefits, and health care.

*Table 3.1* Reasons for remaining in the United Kingdom and self-reported intention to return to Poland

| Categories of answers | Within a few years | | In an indefinite future | | Never | | Hard to say | |
|---|---|---|---|---|---|---|---|---|
| | N | % | N | % | N | % | N | % |
| Prospect of higher earnings | 81 | 56.3 | 91 | 48.9 | 36 | 41.4 | 85 | 41.9 |
| Personal and professional development, better chance of development and advancement | 37 | 25.7 | 63 | 33.9 | 48 | 55.2 | 79 | 38.9 |
| Cultural openness, greater social tolerance | 23 | 16.0 | 36 | 19.4 | 33 | 37.9 | 68 | 33.5 |
| Easier access to the job market | 58 | 40.3 | 63 | 33.9 | 23 | 26.4 | 62 | 30.5 |
| Fears about children's adaptation problems at school in Poland | 20 | 13.9 | 39 | 21.0 | 12 | 13.8 | 38 | 18.7 |
| Better retirement/social benefits and better access to health care than in Poland | 16 | 11.1 | 25 | 13.4 | 17 | 19.5 | 21 | 10.3 |
| Fears about starting a life in Poland almost from scratch | 40 | 27.8 | 82 | 44.1 | 22 | 25.3 | 69 | 34.0 |
| Other reasons | 17 | 11.8 | 10 | 5.4 | 12 | 13.8 | 34 | 16.7 |

*Note*: The figures do not sum up to 100% because respondents were allowed to choose more than one category of answers

Support for these arguments can be found in publications devoted to this subject matter (Titterton, Pelling-Deeves, & Nolan, 2010, p. 3). A relationship was also observed between the continuation of expatriate life due to higher earnings and the time of residence in Britain: the more years of residence away from the country of origin, the lower the strength of the economic argument in favour of staying abroad (<5 years – 59.2%, 5–9 years – 58.3%, 10–14 years – 43.9%, 15–19 years – 44.3%, >20 years – 34.5%). Moreover, the strength of the professional advancement and personal development argument diminished with the decrease in respondents' financial situation (definitely good – 44.3%, fairly good 42.0%, average or rather poor – 30.0%); likewise, the weaker was their command of English, the lower the respondents rated their chance of personal and professional development in the United Kingdom (very good – 50.0%, good – 32.4%, basic conversational – 27.1%, poor or none – 23.7%).

The question about reasons for remaining in Britain had a set of response options which included "fears about starting a life in Poland almost from scratch." When analysing this reason, with the choice of independent variables that we decided to include, we observed a consistent trend indicating that financial situation considerably influenced respondents' intentions: the worse it was in the United Kingdom, the greater were the fears about returning to the country of origin (definitely good – 22.7%, fairly good – 36.0%, average or rather poor – 38.1%).

One of the best developed typologies of return migrants in the literature is Cerase's model. It was built based on migratory behaviours found among the Italians who decided to return from the USA to Italy in the 1960s. Cerase's model includes four types of returns.

- *return of failure*, caused by a failure of the migrant's residence abroad;
- *return of conservatism*, stemming from a conservative approach, return-oriented from the very beginning;
- *return of innovation*, based on an intention of transferring the new experience acquired in the host country to the home country; and
- *return of retirement*, associated with old age plans (Cerase, 1974, pp. 251–254).

In view of this, it was reasonable in our sociological analysis to look for arguments in favour of remaining in the country of settlement for the opposite reasons: failure in the country of origin and/or successes in the country of settlement; non-conservative reasons (return had never been considered); innovation-related reasons – a desire to gain new experience outside the country of origin; and choosing to spend one's old age abroad due to a better social security system.

**Respondents' Reasons for Migrating to Britain Years Ago**

Migration contributes not only to economic and social change but also to a change in individuals' styles of living, thinking, and acting. Polish post-accession migrants often treat their residence in the United Kingdom as a temporary stay to earn money, failing to notice when the time they have spent in the country of settlement is becoming relatively long. In this context, it is worth asking respondents about their reasons for staying in the country of settlement and then juxtapose them with their self-reported reasons for emigrating from Poland to the United Kingdom in the past.

Among the circumstances that induce migrants to seek a "better tomorrow" outside their country of origin, Barbara Sakson distinguished "push" and "pull" factors. The Warsaw-based migration sociologist classified the following as push factors:

- economic factors (high unemployment, bad economic situation of the country, housing and employment difficulties);
- legal factors, demographic factors (too many inhabitants in the productive age); and
- sociopolitical factors (human rights violations, armed conflict, lack of prospects, political situation).

As regards the pull factors, Sakson listed:

- historical factors (historical and cultural connotations);[1]
- economic factors (low unemployment in the host country);
- legal factors (low requirements for foreigners); and
- socioeconomic factors (acceptance of foreigners) (Sakson, 2001, pp. 213–218).

An additional advantage of leaving the country of origin is often mentioned in the literature: the opportunity to travel and explore the world. British sociologist John Urry of Lancaster University even goes as far as suggesting that a distinct sociological discipline should be established, devoted exclusively to the issues of migration networks, mobility, and horizontal fluidity, resulting not only from the currently favourable conditions for movement but also from the speed of information transfer and wide access to information, which have combined to make tourism and travel a desirable and valuable element of contemporary lifestyle (Urry, 2009, p. 15). Although the economic factor remains the main determinant of migration, not all migrants focus solely on escaping poverty, marginalization, or economic problems when deciding to leave the country of origin; through their decision to emigrate, they also seek "a better quality of life" (Cieślińska, 2012, p. 91).

In 2016, Kantar Millward Brown (KMB) research institute published a report titled "Economic Migration of Poles" (a sociological survey on a sample of $N = 671$ respondents, conducted on 4–6 March 2016). The main reason for Poles to emigrate was earnings; higher abroad than in Poland. This reason was indicated by eight in ten respondents (79.0%). The second important argument for them was the higher standards of living in the target host country (59%). Other relatively often indicated arguments included better social conditions (37%), more effective professional development prospects (36%), and the lack of suitable employment in Poland (31%). Compared to the corresponding measurement performed in August 2015, the proportion of respondents who considered emigration due to the higher standards of living abroad increased by 18%, and non-economic arguments, such as the opportunity to travel and explore the world, gained in importance by 21%. It should be noted that the proportion of respondents believing that prospects for development were lacking in Poland decreased by 8% (KMB Kantar Millward Brown, 2016, p. 15).

The sociological research was repeated in March 2018 (Kantar Millward Brown, $N = 708$), and Polish people's migration preferences were analysed again. As previously, eight out of ten Poles who were planning economic emigration decided to leave their country due to earnings (82%). The second most popular factor was the higher standards of living, indicated by more than 36% of respondents, and the third place belonged to social factors (28.6%). Further frequent reasons included the opportunity to travel (23.8%) and better development prospects (24.3%). A marginal reason for emigrating was the lack of employment in Poland, indicated by only 7.7% of respondents (KMB Kantar Millward Brown, 2018b, p. 16).

In September 2018, the Kantar Millward Brown sociological research was conducted again ($N = 593$). In the case of the economic reason, there was a slight decrease – seven out of ten Poles planning economic emigration decided to take this step because of the earnings (68%). Better development prospects and higher standards of living were indicated by every third respondent (32% in both cases), and the "better social conditions" response was one percent less frequent (31%). Every fourth respondent pointed to "a more favourable tax system" as their reason for emigrating; others pointed to more friendly public administration than in the country of origin and to the opportunity to travel and explore the world (24.0% for each of the three answers). In 2018, one of the least significant reasons for emigrating turned out to be unemployment in Poland, indicated by only 14% of respondents, followed by family and loved ones living or planning to live abroad (11%) and a safer geopolitical location (9%) (KMB Kantar Millward Brown, 2018a, p. 16).

In a sociological survey conducted by the Public Opinion Research Centre (CBOS) in November 2019, three-fourths of respondents looking for a job abroad or planning to look for it there in the future reported low earnings in Poland as their reason for leaving the country of origin. Other reasons were indicated occasionally (no percentages are provided in the report cited) (Głowacki, 2019, p. 7).

Considering the literature on the subject and the British determinants of Polish people's migration, in our study we asked respondents why they had decided to emigrate to the United Kingdom and what their key reasons were for deciding to come to the British Isles.

The main reasons for emigrating reported by our respondents were better standards of living in Britain (56.9%) and – related to that – better earnings (49.5%). Every third respondent asserted that they had chosen expatriate life due to the need for change in their life (31.5%), and 28.9% reported that their reason for emigrating had been greater opportunities for self-development, education, and improving professional qualifications (28.9%). The experience of unemployment in Poland forced respondents to leave their country in nearly every fourth case (23.7%), and almost every fifth respondent indicated that what had encouraged them to leave Poland was greater opportunities to travel and explore the world (22.1%) or nostalgia for their loved ones (separation from the family or friends living in Britain – 21.5%). "Other" responses accounted for 4.8% and were centred around two main areas: economic reasons (poverty; the impossibility of maintaining one's family in Poland; lack of prospects for a numerous family in the home country; the possibility of renting a home at a reasonable price; saving money with an intention of returning to Poland; "the Polish government gave me no chance to get out of debt") and family reasons (an English spouse; dual citizenship; help with the grandchildren; emigrating together with the parents; family, etc.) (Table 3.2).

Better living conditions in Britain as compared to Poland had encouraged emigration in the case of six in ten of those respondents who were postponing their return to the home country until some time in the future and in the case of somewhat fewer of those who reported an intention to stay in Britain permanently. Compared to other respondents, the migrants who intended to remain in the country of settlement reported rather rarely that their emigration years before had been due to their financial situation at that time (higher earnings) or due to the need for a change in their life. Respondents planning to stay in Britain after Brexit more often stressed the opportunity to improve their professional qualifications as the main argument that had motivated them when they were leaving the home country.

To sum up, better living conditions abroad were indicated similarly often by men and women as the argument in favour of emigrating to the United Kingdom years before (M = 54.4%, W = 59.6%), but they were considerably more often indicated by respondents in their 30s or 40s (63.9% and 63.4%, respectively), with secondary education (64.4%), blue-collar workers (63.6%), migrants in a fairly good financial situation (62.9%), with a good command of English (65,1%), moderately engaged in the activities of Polish community organisations (64.1%), and having more than nine years of residence abroad (61.5%).

Higher earnings in the country of settlement had made a greater difference at the time of making the migration decision to those individuals who were

*Table 3.2* Reasons for deciding to emigrate to the United Kingdom and self-reported intention to return to Poland

| Categories of answers | Within a few years | | In an indefinite future | | Never | | Hard to say | |
|---|---|---|---|---|---|---|---|---|
| | N | % | N | % | N | % | N | % |
| The experience of unemployment in Poland | 37 | 25.7 | 52 | 28.0 | 19 | 21.8 | 39 | 19.2 |
| Better living conditions | 75 | 52.1 | 113 | 60.8 | 51 | 58.6 | 114 | 56.2 |
| Opportunities for self-development, education abroad, and improving professional or vocational qualifications | 33 | 22.9 | 46 | 24.7 | 36 | 41.4 | 64 | 31.5 |
| Joining the family/friends living in the UK | 28 | 19.4 | 37 | 19.9 | 22 | 25.3 | 46 | 22.7 |
| Higher earnings | 84 | 58.3 | 99 | 53.2 | 38 | 43.7 | 86 | 42.4 |
| Easier access to social welfare | 5 | 3.5 | 4 | 2.2 | 5 | 5.7 | 8 | 3.9 |
| Opportunity to travel and explore the world | 29 | 20.1 | 39 | 21.0 | 20 | 23.0 | 49 | 24.1 |
| A need for change in life | 47 | 32.6 | 61 | 32.8 | 23 | 26.4 | 64 | 31.5 |
| Other | 9 | 6.3 | 2 | 1.1 | 5 | 5.7 | 14 | 6.9 |

*Note:* The figures do not sum up to 100% because respondents were allowed to choose more than one category of answers.

planning to return to Poland at the time of our study (in October 2019). This group is the most numerously represented among men (M = 53.0%, W = 48.2%), respondents in their 30s (65.1%), individuals with secondary education (57.2%), blue-collar workers (61.5%), respondents in a fairly good or poor financial situation (51.9% and 50.5%, respectively), migrants with a basic conversational command of English (58.6%), those with low engagement in Polish community organisations in Britain (54.2%), and those with more than 15 years of residence abroad behind them (57%).

The need for change in life experienced years before was most often reported by respondents determined to return to the home country, respondents over the age of 30 (36.1%), in an average of poor financial situation (36.7%), with a good command of English at the time of the sociological study (35.9%), non-engaged in Polish community organisations in the United Kingdom (38%), and with the shortest history of residence abroad (34.0%).

What is clearly visible at the dawn of contemporary economic migration is a strong economic argument for leaving the country of origin. At the beginning of the new millennium, young migrants set out for Britain and other countries for economic reasons. Our research, conducted in the autumn of 2019, shows that this issue is more complex, however. Migrants' reasons have been evolving towards individual self-fulfilment. In fact, nearly all reasons for emigration, even the economic ones, stem from a higher order need: the need for success, understood in a broad sense.

This observation may be linked with the special nature of post-accession migration, marked by fluidity and unpredictability. Agnieszka Fihel and Izabela Grabowska-Lusińska observe that in the 1990s research into the reasons of migration – both push and pull reasons – was much simpler due to both the quantity and the quality of the phenomenon. While the migrations of that time were mainly caused by economic reasons and return migrations were attributable to the political transformation and its consequences (the motivation being fairly homogeneous), post-accession mobility may elude clear criteria and sociological research tools due to its fluidity and scale (Fihel & Grabowska-Lusińska, 2010, p. 6).

## The Legalisation of Stay in Britain After Brexit

Polish people's migrations to Britain are not a new phenomenon, but their scale and dynamism after 2019 make this area of sociological research a new challenge. At the time when our research was in progress (in the autumn of 2019), there was an ongoing public debate about Brexit scenarios, and respondents learnt about the changing dates of the British Crown's repeatedly rescheduled withdrawal from the European Union. The details of the previously negotiated terms of the agreement between the European Union and the United Kingdom (*deal or no deal*) were not public knowledge at the time. In an atmosphere of general uncertainty associated with Britain's "divorce" from the European

Union, the authorities decided to set the rules concerning EU citizens' further legal stay in Britain. According to the guidelines of the British Home Office, the key requirement was to submit an application for settled status or pre-settled status. The settled status application system for citizens of EU member states living in the United Kingdom was officially launched on 30 March 2019, half a year before the beginning of our quantitative research. The deadline for applying for settled status expired at the end of June 2021. Settled status entitles a person to stay in the United Kingdom without restriction and to apply for British citizenship in the future on condition that they can document at least five years of legal residence. Individuals unable to prove full five years or uninterrupted residence in the United Kingdom at the time of submitting their application will (most probably) be granted pre-settled status; also in this case, however, residence in the United Kingdom must have begun before 31 December 2020 or before the date of Britain's withdrawal from the European Union. These statuses make a person eligible to work legally in the United Kingdom, use public health service, pursue education, or continue studies, receive public funds in the form of pension and other benefits, and travel to and from Britain without restriction (Home Office, 2019).

In direct interviews conducted in 2018 for the National Bank of Poland (NBP), every second respondent met the five-year residence condition (51.0%) and nearly one in three would meet it by the end of 2020. Towards the end of 2018, 29% of respondents reported that they already had permanent residence status, further 21.1% met all formal requirements and had the documents necessary to apply for it. The remaining respondents were those who had not lived in the United Kingdom long enough by the time of the study (32.1%) and those who did not have the documents required to prove the time of their residence (17.9%). In that survey, the individuals who did not meet the length of residence requirement were also asked if they intended to apply for pre-settled or settled status in the United Kingdom. Every third respondent reported uncertainty on this issue (32.6%), slightly fewer answered positively ("yes, I will apply for this status" – 30.5%), every fifth person was not planning to apply for pre-settled or settled status (20.5%), and 16.3% answered that they would apply for it in the future, provided they met the formal requirements (Chmielewska, Panuciak, & Strzelecki, 2019, p. 42).

In a document published by the Home Office, titled "EU Settlement Scheme quarterly statistics, December 2019" and covering all national minorities, the largest number of submitted applications for settled status – 512,310 people – was reported in the case of Poles, and the number of concluded applications was 466,110; settled status was granted in 82% of cases and pre-settled status in 18% of cases. Access to the overall statistical data published by the Home Office, "EU Settlement Scheme: Applications by nationality, region and local authority, 28 August 2018 to 31 December 2019," enabled us to generate figures showing the number of applications submitted in selected urban agglomerations. By the end of 2019, as many as 360,140 Poles applied

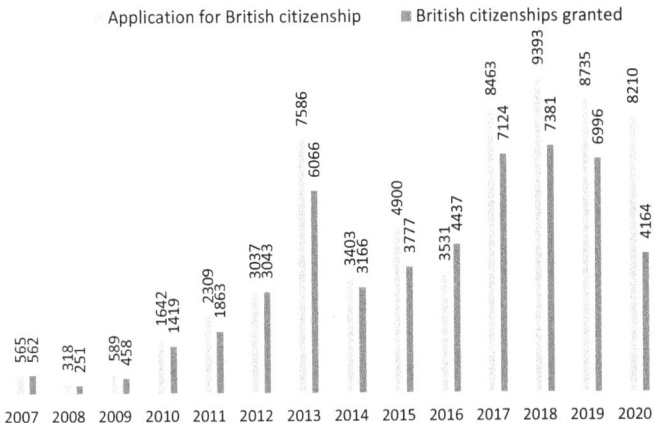

*Figure 3.1* Acquisition of British citizenship by Polish people
*Source*: Immigration Statistics: citizenship (as of 01.08.2022).

for settled status in London (in all districts of Britain's capital city), which accounts for 70.3% of all applications submitted by Poles. There were only 2,750 Polish applicants for settled status in Swindon and 1,750 in Oxford (Home Office, 2020, pp. 6–8). According to the results of the census, the number of people born in Poland who lived in England and Wales amounted to 743,085 in 2021 (Clark, 2023).

Another way of acquiring indefinite leave to remain in the United Kingdom is naturalisation. This policy manifests itself in the naturalisation of foreigners, a widely used practice presupposing that, when applying for citizenship, the immigrant decides to adopt the fundamental values of the United Kingdom's society as their own (Figure 3.1).

Government statistics revealed that the number of Polish citizens obtaining British citizenship peaked in 2017, a year after the Brexit referendum, and in 2013, nine years after Poland's accession to the European Union and the opening of Britain's labour market to immigrants from Poland (Home Office, 2018).

## The Legalisation of Polish People's Stay in the United Kingdom after Brexit: The Results of Our Research

In our survey we asked respondents if they had taken administrative steps that would guarantee their further stay in the United Kingdom after Brexit. Almost half of the respondents reported that they had applied for settled status in Britain (49.1%), two times fewer reported that they intended to apply for it (27.1%), one in ten confirmed having British citizenship (10%), and 4.5% reported that they would not take any action in this regard. Nearly the same number of respondents reported having applied for British citizenship (4.4%), eighteen individuals in the sample were unable to give a specific answer to the question (2.9%), and the rate of missing answers was 1.9% (Table 3.3).

The respondents who had applied for settled status in the United Kingdom were most often those who were planning to return to Poland in an indefinite future and least often those who intended to remain permanently in the British Isles. An intention to apply for settled status was reported by every third respondent planning to return to Poland within a few years and by only one in five of the respondents planning to stay in Britain permanently. The latter most often reported having British citizenship.

Our research shows that Polish migrants who decided to apply for British citizenship were most numerous among respondents in their 40s (45–49 years – 15.3%, 40–44 years – 13.6%) and among those with a master's degree (17.1%) or bachelor's degree (9.3%). At the time when our sociological study was conducted, as many as 17.5% of white-collar workers and only 1.4% of blue-collar workers had British citizenship. The proportion of respondents with British citizenship decreased with the deterioration of their financial situation (definitely good – 15.9%, fairly good – 11.3%, average or rather poor – 7.6%). A tendency was also observed for the number of respondents who had British citizenship to grow with an increase in the length of their residence abroad (5–9 years – 2.1%, 10–14 years – 7.7%, 15–19 years – 21.3%, >20 years – 34.5%).

The respondents who applied for settled status were less often those whose financial situation was average or rather poor (42.2%) than those in a definitely good or fairly good financial situation (52.3% and 55.6%, respectively). The majority of respondents who had come to Britain shortly after the opening of the British labour market in 2004 had already started their settled status application procedure by the time of our study (53.8%). The group that proved to be the most reluctant one to submit application documents was respondents in their 30s. The reason for this may have been the United Kingdom's liberal integration policy at the time, which caused immigrants not to apply for citizenship or settled status (Plewko, 2010, p. 164).

Analysing the overall results of the sociological research conducted in the last few years, one will observe a growing tendency among Poles to apply for settled status in the United Kingdom. There is also an observable proportion of people opting for dual citizenship. The high uncertainty about Brexit certainly contributed to migrants adopting an attitude of waiting to see how the situation would develop and postponing their settled status application.

Contemporary migration researcher Michał P. Garapich draws attention to the abundance of qualitative sociological studies on the reasons why Poles decide to remain in the United Kingdom and to the deficit of quantitative

*Table 3.3* Steps taken to formalize residence in the United Kingdom after Brexit and self-reported intention to return to Poland

| Categories of answers | Within a few years | | In an indefinite future | | Never | | Hard to say | |
|---|---|---|---|---|---|---|---|---|
| | N | % | N | % | N | % | N | % |
| I have applied for settled status in the United Kingdom (through the European Union Settlement Scheme) | 68 | 47.2 | 99 | 53.2 | 38 | 43.7 | 100 | 49.3 |
| I already have British citizenship | 3 | 2.1 | 20 | 10.8 | 16 | 18.4 | 23 | 11.3 |
| I have not taken any steps, but I intend to apply for settled status in the United Kingdom | 49 | 34.0 | 48 | 25.8 | 17 | 19.5 | 54 | 26.6 |
| I have not taken any steps, but I intend to apply for British citizenship | 5 | 3.5 | 4 | 2.2 | 8 | 9.2 | 10 | 4.9 |
| I am not going to take any steps in this regard | 15 | 10.4 | 6 | 3.2 | 2 | 2.3 | 5 | 2.5 |
| Hard to say | 4 | 2.8 | 6 | 3.2 | 4 | 4.6 | 4 | 2.0 |
| No answer | 0 | 0.0 | 3 | 1.6 | 2 | 2.3 | 7 | 3.4 |
| Total | 144 | 100.0 | 186 | 100.0 | 87 | 100.0 | 203 | 100.0 |

$\chi^2 = 44.278$, $df = 15$, $p = 0.000$, $C = 0.261$

empirical studies in this area. The scholar points out that what poses a difficulty is the quantification of answers to the question of why Polish people want to stay in the United Kingdom, because the aim is, above all, to capture the entire context of respondents' life. For this reason, the dominant perspective in studies touching upon this subject is a comparative one with qualitative and ethnographic methods used almost exclusively and quantitative studies lacking (Garapich, 2019, p. 17).

## Summary

In this part of the study, we aimed to review respondents' self-reported intention to remain in Britain after Brexit as reflected in the administrative steps they took to make this possible. What also proved to be interesting from the cognitive point of view is the juxtaposition of Polish people's reasons to stay in the United Kingdom after Brexit with the reasons for coming to the United Kingdom that they had considered when deciding to emigrate. The detailed analysis of empirical data presented makes it possible to formulate certain conclusions about the reasons for choosing to live abroad years ago ("past") and for remaining in the country of settlement after Brexit ("present"); it also leads to certain conclusions regarding the consequence parameter – the extent to which respondents took specific steps to extend their legal residence in the United Kingdom.

Another interesting issue is the correlation of emigration from Poland due to better access to social welfare in the United Kingdom, with the same reason for staying in Britain. This argument was given nearly four times more often as a reason for staying abroad than it was as one of the reasons for emigrating in the past. In the context of the age structure of the surveyed population, it can be said that the Polish diaspora in the United Kingdom is characterised by a considerable predominance of young people (in our sociological study, the 30–39 age band accounted for nearly half of the sample – 44.8%). However, the young migrants by no means disregard the quality of the social and health insurance system in Britain. Although the so-called "peaceful retirement" is a rather distant prospect for them, thinking about social security is an important element in deciding to extend their emigration despite Brexit.

## Note

1  Barbara Cieślińska observes that historical issues are not unimportant to post-accession economic migrants in the United Kingdom; in fact, she argues, "they may even be more important than is commonly believed. Choosing Britain, they go to a country that was close to their compatriots who defended it during World War II. In this case, therefore, Britain's closeness evokes historical and cultural associations" (Cieślińska, 2012, p. 94).

# References

Banaś, Monika. (2005). *Etniczność na sprzedaż*. Kraków: Wydawnictwo Uniwersytetu Jagiellońskiego.

Burrell, Kathy. (2017). *Understanding Polish migration to the UK.* http://www.kathyburrell.net/2017/02/understanding-polish-migration-to-the-uk/#sthash.zyvshl (2020-03-20)

Cerase, Francesco P. (1974). Expectations and reality: A case study of return migration from the United States to Southern Italy. *International Migration Review*, 8 (2), 245–262. https://doi.org/10.1177/019791837400800210 (2023-02-06)

Chmielewska, Iza, Panuciak, Adam, & Strzelecki, Paweł. (2019). *Polacy pracujący za granicą w 2018 r. Raport z badania* (Polski, N. B. Ed.). Warszawa: Departament Statystyki NBP. https://www.nbp.pl/publikacje/migracyjne/polacy_pracujacy_za_granica_2018.pdf (2023-01-12)

Cieślińska, Barbara. (2012). *Emigracje bliskie i dalekie. Studium współczesnych emigracji zarobkowych na przykładzie województwa podlaskiego*. Białystok: Wydawnictwo Uniwersytetu w Białymstoku. https://repozytorium.uwb.edu.pl/jspui/bitstream/11320/7266/1/B_Cieslinska__Emigracje_bliskie_i_dalekie.pdf (2023-02-06)

Clark, Duncan. (2023). *Number of Polish nationals resident in the United Kingdom from 2008 to 2021.* https://www.statista.com/statistics/1061639/polish-population-in-united-kingdom/ (2023-07-14)

Eurostat. (2020). *Average gross annual earnings in industry and services.* https://ec.europa.eu/eurostat (2020-03-30)

Fihel, Agnieszka, & Grabowska-Lusińska, Izabela. (2010). Wstęp. In Grabowska-Lusińska, I. (Ed.), *Poakcesyjne powroty Polaków*, 5–8. Warszawa: Uniwersytet Warszawski. Ośrodek Badań nad Migracjami. https://www.migracje.uw.edu.pl/wp-content/uploads/2016/11/WP_43_101_IGL.pdf (2023-01-06)

Garapich, Michał. (2019). Migracje z Polski do Wielkiej Brytanii: geneza, stan dzisiejszy, wyzwania na przyszłość. *Studia BAS*, 60 (4), 13–30. https://doi.org/10.31268/StudiaBAS.2019.28 (2023-01-06)

Garapich, Michał, & Osipovič, Dorota. (2007). *Migpol. Badanie sondażowe wśród obywateli polskich zamieszkałych w Wielkiej Brytanii i Irlandii. Wrzesień 2007* (Research, M. Ed.). Birmingham: Mig Research. https://docplayer.pl/2804217-Migpol-badanie-sondaowe-wrod-obywateli-polskich-zamieszkalych-w-wielkiej-brytanii-i-irlandii-wrzesie-2007-autorzy.html (2023-02-06)

Głowacki, Antoni. (2019). *Wyjazdy Polaków do pracy za granicę. Komunikat z badań CBOS*, 140/2019, 1–8. Warszawa: Centrum Badania Opinii Społecznej. https://www.cbos.pl/SPISKOM.POL/2019/K_140_19.PDF (2023-01-06)

Grzymała-Moszczyńska, Halina, Grzymała-Moszczyńska, Joanna, Drulik, Joanna, & Szydłowska, Paulina. (2015). *(Nie)łatwe powroty do domu? Funkcjonowanie dzieci i młodzieży powracających z emigracji*. Warszawa: Fundacja Centrum im. prof. Bronisława Geremka. https://www.researchgate.net/publication/321336307_Nielatwe_powroty_do_domu_Funkcjonowanie_dzieci_i_mlodziezy_powracajacych_z_emigracji (2023-06-02)

Home Office. (2018). *Immigration statistics: Citizenship.* https://data.gov.uk/dataset/01da355f-f491-4760-9bbe-8807c8087e37/immigration-statistics-citizenship (2021-10-06)

Home Office. (2019). *Apply to the EU Settlement Scheme (settled and pre-settled status)*. https://www.gov.uk/settled-status-eu-citizens-families/what-settled-and -presettled-status-means (2020-03-30)

Home Office. (2020). *EU Settlement Scheme Quarterly Statistics Home Office Statistical Bulletin*, 5/20, London: Home Office. https://assets.publishing.service.gov.uk/ government/uploads/system/uploads/attachment_data/file/863776/eu-settlement -scheme-statistics-quarterly-december-2019-hosb0520.pdf (2023-05-01)

Iglicka, Krystyna. (2010a). *Powroty Polaków po 2004 roku: w pętli pułapki migracji.* Warszawa: Wydawnictwo Naukowe Scholar.

Iglicka, Krystyna. (2010b). Wyniki badań nad powrotami Polaków przed kryzysem gospodarczym. In Zubik, M. (Ed.), *Poakcesyjne migracje powrotne Polaków: geneza, przyczyny i konsekwencje*, 93–137. Warszawa: Biuro Rzecznika Praw Obywatelskich. https://bip.brpo.gov.pl/pliki/12900036790.pdf (2023-02-06)

Irek, Małgorzata. (2011). *The myth of 'Weak Ties' and the ghost of the Polish peasant: informal networks of Polish post-transition migrants in the UK and Germany* (Vol. 87). Oxford: University of Oxford. https://www.compas.ox.ac.uk/wp-content /uploads/WP-2011-087-Irek_Informal_Networks_Polish_UK_Germany.pdf (2023-01-06)

Karolak, Mateusz. (2015). Migranci powrotni z Wielkiej Brytanii do Polski – przyczyny powrotów z perspektywy biograficznej. *Opuscula Sociologica*, 12 (2), 37–52. https://doi.org/10.18276/os.2015.2-03 (2023-02-06)

KMB Kantar Millward Brown. (2016). *Migracje zarobkowe Polaków IV*, 1–26. Warszawa: Kantar Millward Brown. www.workservice.pl (2020-03-30)

KMB Kantar Millward Brown. (2018a). *Migracje zarobkowe Polaków IX*, 1–26. Warszawa: Kantar Millward Brown. www.workservice.pl (2020-03-30)

KMB Kantar Millward Brown. (2018b). *Migracje zarobkowe Polaków VIII*, 1–30. Warszawa: Kantar Millward Brown. www.workservice.pl (2020-03-30)

Plewko, Jadwiga. (2010). Warunki integracji imigrantów ze społeczeństwem przyjmującym w wybranych krajach Unii Europejskiej. *Roczniki Nauk Społecznych*, 38 (2), 157–180. https://www.ceeol.com/search/viewpdf?id=113206 (2023-02-06)

Pujer, Klaudia. (2017). Poakcesyjne migracje zarobkowe Polaków. In Homoncik, T., Pujer, K., & Wolańska, I. (Eds.), *Ekonomiczno-społeczne aspekty migracji. Wybrane problemy*, 7–31. Wrocław: Exante. https://depot.ceon.pl/bitstream/handle /123456789/11603/migracje_1p.pdf?sequence=1 (2023-01-06)

Rabikowska, Marta. (2010). Negotiation of normality and identity among migrants from Eastern Europe to the United Kingdom after 2004. *Social Identities: Journal for the Study of Race, Nation and Culture*, 16 (3), 285–296. https://doi.org/10.1080 /13504630.2010.482391 (2023-05-01)

Rabikowska, Marta, & Burrell, Kathy. (2009). The material worlds of recent Polish migrants: Transnationalism, food, shops and home. In Burrell, K. (Ed.), *Polish migration to the UK in the 'new' European Union*, 211–232. London: Routledge. https://doi.org/10.4324/9781315601137 (2023-05-01)

Sakson, Barbara. (2001). Źródło pionierskiego łańcucha migracyjnego. In Jaźwińska, E. & Okólski, M. (Eds.), *Ludzie na huśtawce. Migracje między peryferiami Polski i Zachodu*, 204–240. Warszawa: Wydawnictwo Naukowe Scholar.

Slany, Krystyna, & Solga, Brygida. (2014). *Społeczne skutki poakcesyjnych migracji ludności polskich. Raport Komitetu Badań nad Migracjami Polskiej Akademii Nauk* (Nauk, P. A. Ed.). Warszawa: Komitet Badań nad Migracjami Polskiej Akademii

Nauk. https://kbnm.pan.pl/images/Raport_KBnM_PAN_Społeczne_skutki_poakc esyjnych_migracji_ludności_Polski.pdf (2023-01-06)

Szymczak, Wioletta. (2018). Obszary społecznej partycypacji i absencji. In Plewko, J., Szymczak, W., & Adamczyk, T. (Eds.), *Doświadczenie rozwoju w życiu polskich migrantów w Wielkiej Brytanii: praca, rodzina, religijność, partycypacja*, 171–194. Lublin: Towarzystwo Naukowe Katolickiego Uniwersytetu Lubelskiego Jana Pawła II.

Ślebarska, Katarzyna. (2009). Problem bezrobocia w obliczu masowej emigracji zarobkowej. *Śląskie Studia Historyczno-Teologiczne*, 42 (1), 147–156. https:// bazhum.muzhp.pl/media/files/Slaskie_Studia_Historyczno_Teologiczne/Slaskie _Studia_Historyczno_Teologiczne-r2009-t42-n1/Slaskie_Studia_Historyczno _Teologiczne-r2009-t42-n1-s147-156/Slaskie_Studia_Historyczno_Teologiczne -r2009-t42-n1-s147-156.pdf (2023-01-06)

Titterton, Mike, Pelling-Deeves, Sarah, & Nolan, Pauline. (2010). *Usługi i instytucje opieki społecznej w Wielkiej Brytanii. Ekspertyza*. Warszawa: Unia Europejska. https://www.wrzos.org.pl/projekt1.18/download/Ekspertyza%20Anglia.pdf (2023-02-06)

Urry, John. (2009). *Socjologia mobilności*. Warszawa: Wydawnictwo Naukowe PWN.

White, Anne. (2011). *Polish families and migration since EU accession*. Bristol: Bristol University Press. https://doi.org/10.2307/j.ctt9qgmsz (2023.03.25)

Wódka, Marek. (2017). Social and Economic Significance of Moral Capital. *Annales. Etyka w życiu gospodarczym*, 20 (4), 65–75. https://doi.org/10.18778/1899-2226 .20.4.05

# IV  Polish People's Motives for Returning after Brexit

## Introduction

Post-accession migration, particularly to the United Kingdom, has been the subject of numerous analyses and reports, but there are few empirical studies devoted to forecasts on the return migration of Poles in the context of Brexit. The object of the sociological research presented here was Polish migrants living in Britain, with a special focus on post-accession migrants. Let us note, again, that our research was conducted in the autumn of 2019 on a sample of 620 respondents in three historically, demographically, and culturally diverse cities of England: Swindon, with a tradition and history of a typically working-class city; Oxford, as an example of a typical university city; and London, as the largest urban agglomeration, distinguished by its size and by the diversity of social, economic, cultural, and even technical and infrastructural phenomena. In the United Kingdom, cities are the most populous element of the country's spatial structure. A document published by a British government department, the Department for Environment, Food and Rural Affairs, issued in January 2019, reports that in late 2017 and early 2018 only 9.5 million people, accounting for 17% of the country's total population, lived in rural areas and that approximately 495,700 people (0.9% of the population) lived in rural settlements in a sparse setting (Government Statistical Service, 2019, p. 15). Despite the purposeful sampling we applied, this fact allows for making inferences, with some degree of probability, about the whole population of Polish post-accession emigrants in Britain and to forecast future scenarios of economic migration movements.

The main aim of this part of the monograph is to present the diversity of return migration trends and to try to show the reasons behind migrants' decisions to return to Poland, both in the case of individuals planning to return in the near future and in the case of those who do not rule out this decision but are merely postponing it or hesitating on the matter.

## A Review of Current Research on Return Migration

In the qualitative research conducted among migrants returning from the United Kingdom to the south of Poland in the years 2016–2018 (38

DOI: 10.4324/9781003449843-4

questionnaire-based interviews), the authors identified three main types of return migration decisions (Kijonka & Żak, 2020, pp. 128–129):

- planned decisions, connected, for example, with pursuing professional plans or achieving a goal. An analogy can be observed with the concept of "long-time temporariness," consisting of migrants returning to their home country after achieving the goal they had set themselves before emigrating;
- spontaneous decisions, resulting from the sudden emergence of new opportunities or prospects associated with residence in Poland. Decisions of this kind reflect the freedom of movement within the European Union ("intentional unpredictability"), which often results in a characteristic type of migration, highly temporary and unpredictable;
- long-term decisions, which are a consequence of uncertainty about the intention to return to the country of origin. They result in postponing the decision to return.

Spontaneous or long-term decisions were always caused by the emergence of circumstances that forced emigrants to return. These were either objective factors (e.g., deterioration of the financial situation as a result of the world economic crisis) or subjective personal ones (e.g., health problems of the family members who remained in Poland).

In the first half of 2008, the Institute of Public Affairs conducted a survey on a sample of 371 respondents who were in Poland at that time and who had lived in the United Kingdom or Ireland for at least three months in the past ten years. Their main arguments for returning included homesickness (36%), nostalgia for family and friends (29%), temporary or seasonal jobs (18%), and having saved a sufficient amount of money while abroad (18%) (Iglicka, 2010, p. 98). Authors investigating these issues also observed that migration is often linked with the difficult experience of forced separation, uncertain family situations, the weakening of family and social ties, the lack of adequate direct care, and children's school problems. One of the commonly named reasons for returning to the home country is respondents' family situations (Kijonka & Żak, 2020, p. 129). This is confirmed by different research, conducted in connection with Brexit in May and June 2020 using an online survey questionnaire (CAWI), on a sample of 740 return migrants from the United Kingdom. The sample included 525 Poles; the remaining participants were Lithuanians. The key reasons for remigration named by the Poles were nostalgia for the home country (36.4%), longing for the family and the loved ones (25.5%), the need to bring up the children in the country of origin (24.8%), and the need to look after family members living in the country of origin (22.3%) (Czeranowska & Wermińska-Wiśnicka, 2021, p. 185).

## Polish People's Reasons for Returning: The Results of Our Research

In the last quarter of 2019, there were many indications that the House of Commons in the British Parliament would implement the "hard Brexit" scenario, which meant the United Kingdom leaving the European Union without any withdrawal agreement. This would have had numerous consequences, both for the European Union and for the United Kingdom, which is why this problem became the "number one topic" in the mass media in Britain and worldwide. This was the sociopolitical context in which we conducted research among Polish migrants in Britain in the autumn of 2019. In that research, we asked respondents about their reasons for returning to Poland. Our statistical analysis included both respondents who were already determined at the time of the study to leave the United Kingdom and return to Poland and those who had not yet decided to take this step but were considering it as an option.

Our study indicated that the main argument for returning to the home country was the experience of separation from one's family and the weakening of ties with loved ones (46%). Every third respondent reported that a strong reason inducing them to remigrate was nostalgia for the home country (30.5%). Every fifth respondent indicated that what encouraged them to make this decision was the improved standards of living in Poland (21.3%) and the vanishing of Polish culture, customs, and traditions during their life abroad – the latter argument was indicated by 19% of respondents. Slightly less often, migrants reported other reasons for returning to Poland, such as: the multicultural clash in Britain manifesting itself in ideological incompatibility and a conflict of values (17.6%), the guarantee of their children getting religious education in Poland (12.6%), a bodily injury or health impairment (2.7%), and other reasons (4.5%). The arguments in the "other reasons" category were usually financial stability in Poland thanks to British pensions and a sense of having achieved economic security regarding the resources collected/earned. According to current legislation, Poles should have worked for a required time in the United Kingdom to be able to apply to the United Kingdom's insurance body, the Department for Work and Pensions, for a pension calculation, which they may be entitled to even if they return to Poland (Table 4.1).

Separation from the family became the strongest reason to return for two-thirds of those who were planning to leave Britain within the nearest few years. This argument also proved to be crucial to those who reported an intention to remain in Britain after Brexit: should they choose to return to Poland, this would also be their reason for returning.

Another argument for returning to Poland, the next in the hierarchy of importance, was nostalgia for the home country. This was more often stressed by those who had decided to return to Poland within a few years (46.5%) and

Table 4.1 Main reasons for returning to Poland and declared time of return

| Categories of answers | Within a few years | | In an indefinite future | | Never | | Hard to say | |
|---|---|---|---|---|---|---|---|---|
| | N | % | N | % | N | % | N | % |
| Separation from the family / weakening family ties | 96 | 66.7 | 109 | 58.6 | 13 | 14.9 | 67 | 33 |
| Disappearance of Polish culture, customs, and traditions | 48 | 33.3 | 41 | 22 | 8 | 9.2 | 21 | 10.3 |
| A bodily injury or health impairment | 6 | 4.2 | 6 | 3.2 | 2 | 2.3 | 3 | 1.5 |
| Improved standards of living in Poland | 55 | 38.2 | 44 | 23.7 | 3 | 3.4 | 30 | 14.8 |
| Guarantee of children's religious education | 38 | 26.4 | 22 | 11.8 | 2 | 2.3 | 16 | 7.9 |
| Nostalgia, longing for the home country | 67 | 46.5 | 79 | 42.5 | 4 | 4.6 | 39 | 19.2 |
| The multicultural clash in Britain, ideological incompatibility, conflict of values | 46 | 31.9 | 33 | 17.7 | 3 | 3.4 | 27 | 13.3 |
| Other | 6 | 4.2 | 8 | 4.3 | 4 | 4.6 | 10 | 4.9 |

*Note*: The figures do not sum up to 100% because respondents were allowed to choose more than one category of answers.

in an indefinite future (42.5%) and less often by respondents who were unde-cided about returning (19.2%).

Nearly four out of ten migrants determined to return to Poland within a few years and almost every fourth migrant planning to return in an indefinite future (38.2% and 23.7%, respectively) reported that they were doing so for economic reasons and that the improved standards of living in Poland was what encouraged them to return.

Separation from family as the reason for returning to Poland was most often indicated by women (W = 58.9%, M = 44.1%), individuals under the age of 30 (67.9%), and respondents with general secondary, technical secondary, or post-secondary education (57.8%). Longing for the family, as an argument for returning, became stronger in proportion to the decrease in respondents' financial situation (definitely good – 48.7%, fairly good – 50.7%, average or rather poor – 57.4%). Activity in Polish community organisations usually compensated for this longing in the case of individuals reporting high engage-ment or engagement compared to those reporting medium or low engagement and to non-engaged ones (46.7% and 50% versus 56.2%, 52%, and 55.6%, respectively). The respondents who reported an intention to return to Poland due to the weakening of family ties were more often those who had arrived in Britain between 2010 and 2014 and the youngest migrants, with up to five years of residence in the United Kingdom (67% and 62.4%, respectively). Almost every second respondent who had lived abroad for 10–14 years (51.2%) or slightly longer (15–19 years – 49%) expressed a longing for their closest family members.

Nostalgia for the home country was most frequently experienced by respondents reporting an intention to return to Poland. It was reported by every third man (34.9%) and slightly more women (36%), and most often by the oldest participants in the sociological survey (≥50 years – 47.5%). However, it was only cited by one in five of the youngest migrants, and most often by respondents with a master's degree (36.6%). Nostalgia for the home country as the reason for returning to Poland was more often reported by blue-collar workers than by white-collar ones (38.8% versus 32.4%), by respond-ents with a comparatively weaker command of English (basic conversational – 41%, poor or none – 41%, good – 37.2%, very good – 29.1%), and by those who had come to Britain before 1999 (41.7%), and less often by respondents who had lived abroad for up to five years (31.8%). Longing for the home country increased with the deterioration of the respondents' financial situation (definitely good – 25.6%, fairly good – 34.1, average or rather poor – 40.4%).

The improvement of the standards of living in Poland became an argument for returning mainly in the group of respondents determined to take this step. This argument was indicated by every third man (29.7%) and every fourth woman (21.5%); it was indicated more often by older emigrants (≥50 years – 30.5%, 45–49 years – 34) and by those respondents who had arrived in the United Kingdom the earliest (41.7%), than by those who had chosen expatriate life up to five years before (20%). It is hardly surprising that improved standards of living in Poland as an argument for returning to the home country became more frequent with the deterioration of respondents' financial situation abroad (definitely good – 16.7%, fairly good – 20.6%, average or rather poor – 31.9%). Also visible is a decrease in the percentage of migrants willing to return to Poland because of the improved standards of living there in the case of well-educated respondents (primary or basic vocational education – 30.8%; general secondary, technical secondary, or post-secondary education – 27.6%; bachelor's degree – 23.1%; master's degree – 21.8%). Those who had a better command of English less often considered better living standards in the country of origin as an argument for returning (good English – 24%, very good English – 21.4%).

## Discussion and an Attempt at a Forecast

Based on the data concerning the causes of Polish people's return migration, collected and presented in the previous paragraphs, it must be concluded that in the examined population the study revealed no returns of innovation, which are the most important from the point of view of the possible social change that such people could initiate after returning from abroad (Iglicka, 2010, p. 123). Our research has also revealed that at least one-fourth of the Poles could be expected to return within a few years after Brexit, and that in the long-term perspective as many as half of the Polish migrants may decide to remigrate.

As regards specific categories of quantitative data, it is worth highlighting that blue-collar workers tend to be more willing to return to Poland than white-collar workers. This difference was found for all time bands – among respondents reporting an intention to return within a year, within a few years, and in an indefinite future. This phenomenon can be seen as resulting from the increase in the earnings of blue-collar workers in Poland. Data collected by Statistics Poland (GUS) show that between 2004 and 2010 this increase was highest among technicians and associate professionals (55.9%), service and sales workers (54.8%), and elementary workers (53.3%) (Broniatowska, Majchrowska, & Żółkiewski, 2013, p. 105).

Two contrary tendencies can be seen in the case of migrants whose financial situation was the best – one should be considered in terms of change and the other in terms of continuity. It turns out that among the migrants who wanted to leave Britain as soon as possible there were those who evaluated their financial situation as definitely good or good. An almost identical proportion of respondents in a very good or good financial situation did not want to leave the British Isles. In both situations, the type of migration can be classified as unilaterally open or bilaterally closed (Szymczak, 2018, pp. 24–25), though the goals of emigration seem to be diametrically different. In the former case, the self-reported intention to return to Poland can be interpreted as caused by the migrant having improved his or her financial situation, while in the latter case the intention to return should be explicated as a consequence of the goal – previously set and subsequently verified – of improving one's situation in life abroad as an alternative to life in the country of origin.

The percent of respondents reporting an intention to return to Poland "in an indefinite future" increased with their deteriorating financial situation, which can be explained by the fact that their financial situation abroad had not yet reached the level they expected it to reach. They postponed their departure, calculating that their chance of improving their financial situation was still greater abroad than in the country of origin.

Our research also showed that the respondents thinking about leaving Britain were more often those whose English was not particularly good. It can be assumed that command of English is one of the elements of migrants' assimilation in the country of settlement. The language barrier makes it more difficult to freely engage in communication, form relationships, and, finally, participate in the social, economic, political, and cultural life of that country. Ignorance of the language prevents integration and makes it impossible for the immigrants to blur all kinds of borders separating them from the society of the host country, let alone "blend into" that society (Włodarczak, 2005, p. 5).

It should also be noted that as many as one-third of the respondents with the shortest time of residence in the United Kingdom, belonging to the first three lengths of residence categories, reported an intention to return to Poland in an indefinite future (<5 years – 31.1%, 5–9 years – 32%, 10–15 years – 30.4%). These were individuals who had no specific plans for the immediate future and were not determined to return to Poland "at all costs." It is them that the future form of the Polish community in Britain will undoubtedly depend on. Moreover, every third emigrant in the oldest group and every tenth respondent in the youngest group were not planning to return to Poland.

## Summary

Certain trends can be identified in the issues analysed in this part of the monograph, both in the group of returning migrants and in the group of remaining ones. Longing and nostalgia for the home country are experienced to an almost equal degree by those who plan to return and by those who plan to remain. Migrants planning to remain in Britain do not experience the disappearance of Polish culture, traditions, and customs while living abroad as strongly as do those planning to return. The guarantee of children's religious upbringing is a strong argument encouraging the Poles to return (Wódka, Fel, & Kozak, 2020); the migrants who intend to remain in the United Kingdom do not attach great importance to this argument, however. Likewise, returnees perceive a conflict between their values and those represented in a multicultural society; respondents planning to remain in the United Kingdom after Brexit do not share this sentiment.

Poles continue to be one of the largest national minorities in the United Kingdom. Unfortunately, the prospects regarding the future form of the Polish diaspora do not seem to be optimistic. A sudden wave of return migrations should probably not be expected in the nearest years, but it can be predicted, with a high degree of probability, that half of professionally active Poles may sooner or later return to their country of origin. The scale of these returns will largely depend on the now undecided individuals, whose "remain or return" dilemma is set in the current experience of uncertainty about professional stability in the job market in Britain and, potentially, in Poland. These people lack a clearly defined prospect, cannot plan their future, and therefore feel, in a way, at risk of social degradation (Standing, 2014, p. 65).

## References

Broniatowska, Paulina, Majchrowska, Aleksandra, & Żółkiewski, Zbigniew. (2013). Wynagrodzenie minimalne w Polsce. Czy powinno być zróżnicowane regionalnie? *Studia BAS Biura Analiz Sejmowych Kancelarii Sejmu*, 4, 97–124. https://depot .ceon.pl/handle/123456789/12246 (2022-03-26)

Czeranowska, Olga, & Wermińska-Wiśnicka, Iga. (2021). Nostalgiczne powroty Polaków i Litwinów w kontekście brexitu i pandemii. *Zmiana społeczna, pandemia i kryzys. Konteksty empiryczne i teoretyczne*, 1, 171–198. https://www.researchgate .net/publication/353378365_Nostalgiczne_powroty_Polakow_i_Litwinow_w _kontekscie_brexitu_i_pandemii_Nota_badawcza_na_podstawie_wynikow _sondazu_porownawczego_na_probie_litewskich_oraz_polskich_migrantow _powracajacych_z_Wielkiej_B (2023-02-06)

Goverment Statistical Service. (2019). *Statistical Digest of Rural England*, 1–22. London: Department for Environment Food and Rural Affairs. https://assets .publishing.service.gov.uk/government/uploads/system/uploads/attachment_data /file/1002686/06_Statistical_Digest_of_Rural_England_2019_June_edition.pdf (2023-02-06)

Iglicka, Krystyna. (2010). Wyniki badań nad powrotami Polaków przed kryzysem gospodarczym. In Zubik, M. (Ed.), *Poakcesyjne migracje powrotne Polaków: geneza, przyczyny i konsekwencje*, 93–137. Warszawa: Biuro Rzecznika Praw Obywatelskich. https://bip.brpo.gov.pl/pliki/12900036790.pdf (2023-02-06)

Kijonka, Justyna, & Żak, Monika. (2020). Polish return migrants: Analysis of selected decision-making processes. *Studia Migracyjne - Przegląd Polonijny*, 178 (4), 115–136. https://doi.org/10.4467/25444972SMPP.2041.12778 (2023-05-01)

Standing, Guy. (2014). *Prekariat: Nowa niebezpieczna klasa*. Warszawa: Wydawnictwo Naukowe PWN. https://www.ce.uw.edu.pl/wp-content/uploads/2017/10/5.-guy -standing_nowa-niebezpieczna-klasa.pdf (2023-02-06)

Szymczak, Wioletta. (2018). Obszary społecznej partycypacji i absencji. In Plewko, J., Szymczak, W., & Adamczyk, T. (Eds.), *Doświadczenie rozwoju w życiu polskich migrantów w Wielkiej Brytanii: praca, rodzina, religijność, partycypacja*, 171–194. Lublin: Towarzystwo Naukowe Katolickiego Uniwersytetu Lubelskiego Jana Pawła II.

Włodarczak, Krystyna. (2005). *Proces adaptacji współczesnych emigrantów polskich do życia w Australii Prace Migracyjne*, 1–71. Warszawa: CMR Working Papers.

https://www.migracje.uw.edu.pl/wp-content/uploads/2016/12/003_61.pdf (2023-01-06)

Wódka, Marek, Fel, Stanisław, & Kozak, Jarosław. (2020). Religiosity of Polish Catholics in the UK: Attitude towards faith, affiliation, membership and religious practices. *Religions*, 11 (8), 1–13. https://doi.org/10.3390/rel11080422 (2023-02-15)

# V Conclusion

Migration is becoming a common phenomenon, involving people of all ages and different genders, diverse in terms of place of residence, personal situation, education level, qualifications, and professional as well as financial situation. Contemporary social mobility has become a repeatable, circular phenomenon. Migration is creating a new kind of liquidity (Bauman, 2006, p. 231); it is becoming a new type of nomadism and a hallmark of the postmodern lifestyle.

This kind of perspective on migration gave rise to the authors' interest in one of the aspects of Polish people's migration – namely, the situation of Polish migrants in Britain in the context of Brexit. This interest took the form of sociological research aimed at finding an answer to the question of how Polish migrants in the United Kingdom interpreted and perceived their further stay there in the context of the ongoing Brexit process, including how they viewed their current membership in the Polish diaspora and how they perceived Brexit and its possible consequences. What became the central point of the analysis presented in this book was the dilemma manifesting itself in migrants' decision to stay abroad or return from emigration.

Our intention was to present, or at least outline, the attitudes of the Poles living in the United Kingdom towards Brexit. We attempted to determine the reasons migrants choose to stay in Britain or return to Poland after years spent in the country of settlement. Moreover, we sought answers to the questions of what changes, if any, in Polish people's consciousness resulted from British citizens' Brexit decision, what changes occurred in the knowledge and opinions of Poles in Britain on the sociopolitical transformations taking place in that country, and how they evaluated the media coverage of and the preparations for Britain's withdrawal from the European Union.

Based on research results, in the first chapter, we have sketched a portrait of a young Polish emigrant who lives abroad and has found themselves in what is, to some extent, a forced situation, in which they have to make important decisions between the options of staying in the country of settlement and returning to the country of origin.

In the second chapter, we have shown how migrants perceive Brexit and its consequences, particularly what opinions they have about the

DOI: 10.4324/9781003449843-5

communication of Brexit-related information by Polish and British authorities, Britain's preparation for leaving the European Union, and the possible consequences of Brexit (gains or losses) not only for the United Kingdom, Poland, and Europe but also for the respondent and their family. The large majority of respondents reported a belief that leaving the European Union would have a detrimental effect. The sentiment that prevailed in answers about the possible benefits or negative consequences of Brexit for the European Union, the United Kingdom, Poland, and the respondent was anxiety about the effects of the Brexit departure. It should be noted, however, that respondents looking at Brexit optimistically were also considerably numerous.

The effects of Brexit prove to be extremely difficult to predict because this process should be viewed as one that extends to many domains of everyday life. The United Kingdom's departure from the European Union will have numerous consequences which, though hard to predict, are present in the consciousness of British people themselves and migrants in Britain. Britain's "divorce" from the European Union will undoubtedly also change the situation of the Poles who have chosen a life of migrants in that country and will make leaving Poland more difficult for those who have been planning to emigrate in the years to come. Currently, it is difficult to estimate how exactly the status of Polish migrants living in Britain will change. Many experts claim that, given the restrictions that present and future migrants may encounter, the likelihood of their return to Poland can be expected to increase due to social unrest caused by the uncertain socioeconomic and political situation between the European Union and the United Kingdom.

The third and fourth parts of the book are devoted to the topic of Polish people returning to their homeland on the Vistula or remaining in the country on the Thames. The primary issue in these chapters is dilemmas associated with the motives for returning or staying, as the results of the referendum came as a surprise to many migrants. Brexit put a question mark on the rights acquired by migrants concerning many spheres of their life, such as the right to move freely, to work, and to pursue education. This situation certainly became a challenge for the Poles living in Britain, who had never before been forced to make the final decision about settlement or departure; Brexit undoubtedly intensified their reflection on this dilemma.

In this study, self-reported plans of returning to Poland or staying permanently in Britain are a variable of fundamental significance. The largest group in the sample were individuals who were still hesitating about whether to stay permanently in the country of settlement or to return to their country of origin (32.7%). An intention to return to Poland within an unspecified time frame was reported by 30% of respondents. Nearly one in five respondents reported an intention to return to Poland within a year or within a few years (23.2%), whereas one person in seven answered that they intended to stay in Britain permanently (14.1%).

In further analysis, we decided not to maintain the statistical order when describing the examined community because the largest group was undecided respondents. In this fragment of the book, we therefore adopted a structure of statistical description that reflected the order of the categories of answers – those who intended to return to their country of origin ("within a few years"; "in an indefinite future"), those who intended to stay permanently in the country of settlement ("never"), and those who had not made any decision on returning or staying by the time of the survey ("hard to say") (Figure 5.1).

The group of respondents reporting an intention to return to Poland as soon as possible included more women than men (M = 42.1%, W = 57.9%). It was composed of respondents in their 30s (43.4%), with general secondary, technical secondary, or post-secondary education (38%), blue-collar workers (62.4%), the same percent of respondents reporting a fairly good and average or rather poor financial situation (39.4% in both cases), individuals with a good command of English (35.9%), and those who had lived abroad for 10–20 years (51.1%) or for a shorter time (less than ten years – 47.5%).

Among those who were thinking of returning from the United Kingdom to Poland but were postponing this return, there were nearly two times more women than men (M = 37.7%, W = 62.3%); this group included the largest proportion of people in their 30s (43%), comparable proportions of respondents with secondary education (35.9%) and with a master's degree (34.8%), similar numbers of blue-collar and white-collar workers (54.4% versus 45.6%), and mostly individuals who were not particularly well-off (financial

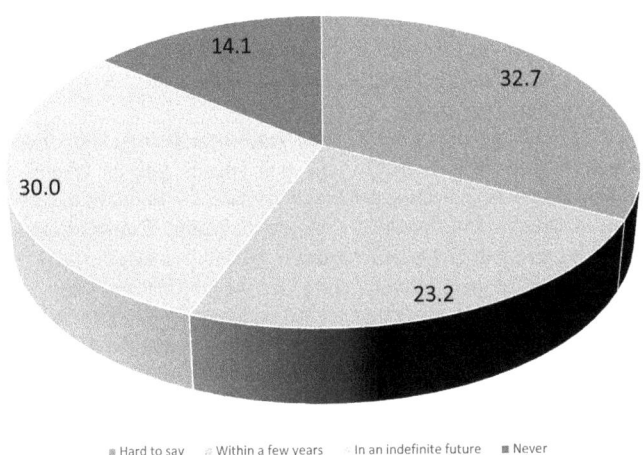

■ Hard to say    ◌ Within a few years    ○ In an indefinite future    ■ Never

*Figure 5.1* Plans of returning to Poland or staying in Britain (data in %)

situation: definitely good – 12.4%, fairly good – 41.2%, average or rather poor – 46.5%). Respondents planning to return to Poland in an indefinite future were characterised by a good command of English (very good – 32.2%, good – 36.1%, basic conversational – 23.5%, poor or none – 8.2%). The majority of the participants in this group had lived in Britain for 10–20 years at the time when our sociological research was conducted.

Respondents planning to stay permanently in the United Kingdom were predominantly women (M = 27.1%, W = 72.9%), individuals in their 30s (39%), reporting higher (41.2%) or secondary (35.3%) education, white-collar workers (64.4%), in a good financial situation (57%), with a very good command of English (63.5%), with 10–20 years of residence in the United Kingdom behind them (62.7%).

Those who had no clear position on returning or staying in Britain were also predominantly women (65.6%), people in their 30s (49.5%) and 40s (33.2%), well-educated (master's degree – 43.3%), with a slight prevalence of white-collar workers over blue-collar ones (53.6% versus 46.4%); most of them were in a good financial situation (53%) and were effective users of the language of the country of settlement (command of English: very good: – 37.4%, good – 39%, basic conversational – 18.5%, poor or none – 5.1%). Of the respondents who were undecided about returning or staying in the United Kingdom, 72.5% had lived there for 10–20 years.

So far, one of the characteristic features of Polish migrants in Britain has been its "intentional unpredictability." Migrants often tried to keep their options open, observing the changing conditions both in the country of origin and in the one they had migrated to, constantly checking the opportunities available (Szkudlarek, 2019). It should be assumed that even though many migrants still report hesitation about their plans, the unstable situation associated with Brexit and the bleak prospect of their current rights being restricted will force most of them to formulate more specific declarations or to rethink their current life and revise their plans of staying in the United Kingdom or returning to their country of origin.

It turned out that the respondents' main reason for leaving the United Kingdom was longing for their family. This corresponds with the results of other sociological studies, indicating that family continues to be one of the most highly regarded values in Polish people's axiological system. The second most often reported argument in favour of returning to Poland was longing and nostalgia for the country of origin, and the third was the respondents' subjective evaluation concerning the improvement in the standards of living in Poland. Further circumstances that argued in favour of returning were the disappearance of Polish culture and customs, the axiological conflict resulting from the multicultural character of British society that respondents had experienced, and the guarantee of their children getting better religious education in Poland.

An interesting finding is the correlation between migrants' current financial situation and specific reasons for returning to their country of origin. It turns out that their economic situation compensates for the longing they feel for their family. As a result, those who were better off abroad less often indicated this particular reason for returning to Poland. Economic and rational reasons may have had an impact here. Unsatisfactory living conditions in the country of origin, a gulf between expectations and current reality, perhaps a growing dissatisfaction with the standards of living in Poland, and reluctance to live in a reality that did not offer positive prospects for the future led to the rationalisation of plans to return to Poland, including a feeling of nostalgia for the homeland. The reverse tendency was observed in individuals experiencing disappointment with migration, which failed to sufficiently compensate for leaving Poland, for example by improving their financial situation. The improvement of the economic situation in Poland was more often indicated as the reason for considering return by those migrants whose economic situation was not particularly good. We observed a pattern of nostalgia for Poland increasing with the deterioration of the financial situation, which became a serious argument in favour of considering return, especially in respondents disappointed with the opportunities for a better life abroad. This attests, once again, to the power of the economic argument.

Also noteworthy are the research results concerning the acculturation and assimilation of migrants in the environment in which they have come to live. A poor command or ignorance of the language used in the place of settlement contributed to inadequate integration into the current place of residence and, consequently, to a stronger experience of nostalgia for the home country and longing for the loved ones. This fact can be explained by a sense of "rejection" by the host country, manifesting itself in a lack of assimilation or integration into the local community. What becomes visible in this context is the meaning and role of Polish community organisations. Longing for the loved ones was least often experienced by those respondents who engaged in the activities of such organisations bringing compatriots together. It should be noted that the sense that the culture and customs associated with the Polish tradition were disappearing clearly diminished with an increase in the number of years spent away from the home country.

An important argument, though not the primary one, when considering departure from the country of settlement was respondents' concern for the religious education of their children. Concern for their children's proper religious education was most frequently cited as a reason to return to Poland among respondents in their 30s and least frequently in extreme age groups (the youngest and the oldest participants) in the study. It can be assumed that the reason this concern was most often expressed by respondents aged 30–39 at the time of the study was that this problem directly concerned their families. In the extreme age bands – both over the age of 50 and under the age of 30 – the religious education dilemma very likely no longer concerned the respondents or did not concern them yet.

The vast majority of the Poles taking part in the study felt safe in Britain. They did not expect Brexit to have drastically negative consequences for them. Many of them reported an intention to stay in the United Kingdom or to return to Poland in an indefinite time frame. The latter does not necessarily mean actual willingness to return to the country of origin. It may as well indicate an attitude of "not burning one's bridges." In this case, this may mean that the number of people staying permanently in Britain is not going to not fall drastically in the nearest few years. Another possibility is an increase in circular migrations – an attempt to combine two centres of life: the country of settlement and the country of origin.

Brexit and its possible implications in the sphere of employment did not stir anxiety among economic migrants. The effects of British citizens' decision to leave the European Union did not cause social panic resulting from fears that salaries might be reduced and that, consequently, migrants' standard of living might deteriorate. What is more, compared to the time of their arrival years before, respondents perceived greater opportunities for self-development in Britain after Brexit. Instead of undermining the belief in greater opportunities there (e.g., opportunities to improve professional qualifications), the spectre of Britain's withdrawal from the European Union actually strengthened that belief. This finding is all the more interesting as during our research the respondents had no knowledge of how, after the transitional period was over, Brexit agreements would regulate the recognition of professional qualifications acquired outside the United Kingdom.

Brexit is undoubtedly an unprecedented event that will mark an important point in the history of the European Union and significantly influence its position in the international environment. It will lead to relatively big changes and transformations in the lives of people whose lifestyle so far has been associated with stability in many areas. Britain's departure from the European Union will also undoubtedly change the situation of the Poles who have chosen the life of migrants in that country and will make leaving the country of origin more difficult for those who have been planning to emigrate to the United Kingdom in the years to come. Despite the fears associated with post-Brexit changes, many people take on this challenge and choose to continue their life abroad in the future. It should be stressed that both decisions to return and decisions to stay are marked by hope for a better life. This ambition essentially stems from individuals' aspirations to develop, even if this is not clearly stated in their argumentation for staying or returning.

Let us stress once again that, even though it is currently difficult to estimate how exactly the status of Polish migrants living in Britain will change, given the barriers that future migrants may face, the probability of the Polish diaspora in that country becoming smaller is increasing. It can also be expected that the situation will be further complicated by the consequences of the COVID-19 pandemic and by the uncertainty resulting from the war in Ukraine.

# References

Bauman, Zygmunt. (2006). *Płynna nowoczesność*. Kraków: Wydawnictwo Literackie.
Szkudlarek, Aleksandra. (2019). *Brexit i co dalej? Dylematy polskich migrantów poakcesyjnych w Wielkiej Brytanii*. Warszawa: Instytut Socjologii UW. https://www.migracje.uw.edu.pl/wp-content/uploads/2019/06/WP117175.pdf (2023-02-06)

# Index

For Product Safety Concerns and Information please contact our EU
representative GPSR@taylorandfrancis.com
Taylor & Francis Verlag GmbH, Kaufingerstraße 24, 80331 München, Germany

www.ingramcontent.com/pod-product-compliance
Ingram Content Group UK Ltd.
Pitfield, Milton Keynes, MK11 3LW, UK
UKHW020027260325
456732UK00013B/80